SHOOT LOW, BOYS— THEY'RE RIDIN' SHETLAND PONIES

LEWIS GRIZZARD
In Search Of True Grit

PEACHTREE PUBLISHERS, LTD.

Published by
PEACHTREE PUBLISHERS, LTD.
494 Armour Circle, N.E.
Atlanta, Georgia 30324

Manufactured in the United States of America

1st Printing

Library of Congress Catalog Number 85-61974

ISBN 0-931948-79-7

To Chuck Perry, the editor's editor.

— 1 —

Walk a Mile
In the Duke's Boots

HERO. IT WAS a word I heard often in my youth. Even before I knew what it meant, what it stood for, I liked the way it sounded. HEro, as in strong and masculine. You almost grit your teeth as it rushes from the back of the mouth.

I think the first time I heard it used was in reference to my father. He was recently back from Korea, where he had been wounded and captured before escaping and being sent home. All the men who fought that war were heroes, but my father's Purple Heart certified his status.

I remember sitting in his lap with my arm around his neck and feeling the back of his head. "What are these lumps, Daddy?" I asked.

"Shrapnel," he said.

"What's that?"

He tried to explain. It all sounded so exciting, so heroic,

1

to a five-year-old boy. He never complained about the pain, but my mother said he used to get awful headaches. Maybe the booze helped to ease that pain. And when it beat him down and left him in ruin, they called him "hero" again as a sort of explanation. It was years before I knew what they meant.

The next hero I encountered was Roy Rogers. At age six I saw my first Roy Rogers movie, and afterwards I rode with him and Trigger and Bullet and Dale and Buttermilk on a thousand vicarious adventures through the woods near my house and once even into my mother's flower garden.

"Get out of that flower garden!" my mother screamed.

"Quiet, Mom," I whispered back. "They're about to rob the stage."

My grandfather (who was quite heroic to me, too, since all the neighborhood dogs followed him around) was also a big Roy Rogers fan. Once when we were watching Roy on TV, a collection of range riffraff kidnapped Dale and took her to the line shack. I never knew exactly what a line shack was, but there was always one in every western, and nothing good ever happened there.

As the villains tied up Dale, my grandfather yelled to the television screen, "Don't worry, Dale! Roy'll get those sons of bitches!" Which he most certainly did.

Years later I had the opportunity to interview Dale Evans, and I asked her whatever became of Trigger and Bullet. "Roy had them stuffed and put into his museum when they died," she said.

For Dale's sake, I hope Roy goes before she does.

Norris Cole was another of my early heroes. He was a year older than me and one of the greatest climbers of all time. After observing that squirrels had unusually long claws which enabled them to climb trees with ease, Norris grew his fingernails and toenails extremely long. He soon became known as Norris "Claws" Cole.

"Claws is a real good climber," his little brother Fred used to say, "but he's awful to sleep with." About twice a month Fred would have to go to the doctor for stitches after Claws had rolled over during the night and snared him. Fred eventually took to sleeping with the dogs.

Claws didn't care how tall a thing was or how much danger was involved; if it was there, he climbed it. Trees were his specialty, but he also climbed the town water tank, Confederate war memorials, forest ranger towers, the Methodist church steeple and every telephone pole in town.

All of his climbing wasn't recreational, however; he also did public service climbing. Mrs. Loot Starkins's husband, Jake, used to get very drunk, and when Mrs. Loot started screaming at him, Jake would climb to the top of the tree in their front yard to get away from her. One day Mrs. Loot screamed so much that Jake, perched safely in his tree, swore he was never coming down again. Somebody called for Claws, and he climbed up and talked Jake down out of the tree.

"How'd you do it?" one of the neighbor ladies asked.

"Told him if he didn't come down, I was going to teach Mrs. Loot how to come up," said Claws.

I heard several years ago that Claws died in a climbing accident, although more than likely it was the falling that got him.

"Reckon Claws went to heaven?" one of the locals asked when he heard about the accident.

"If they tried to keep him out," said an old man, "he'd just

3

climb right back in."

Then, of course, there was my boyhood friend and idol, Weyman C. Wannamaker, Jr., a great American in the truest sense of the phrase. It was Weyman, for example, who taught me to shoot pool and to use the big end of the cue to hit folks over the head with in case of a disagreement.

"You had one foot off the floor when you made that shot," an unwise opponent said to Weyman one afternoon in the pool hall. Words were exchanged, and then the other fellow called Weyman a "do-do pot who doesn't love the Lord."

Weyman turned his cuestick around and raised a large lump on the head of the source of the insult. Then he pulled the victim's mouth open and inserted the five-ball. Afterwards, Weyman could have climbed onto the table and kicked balls into the pockets, and no one would have spoken on behalf of the rules of billiards. A man has to do what he has to do.

There was almost no end to Weyman's talents and his heroism. His most heroic act, however, was single-handedly removing the snake from Kathy Sue Loudermilk's dress. Of course, it was Weyman who put it there in the first place. A man has to do what he has to do.

It was just a little garden snake, but after Kathy Sue flailed around for awhile, screaming and shrieking, Weyman began to feel guilty. So he pushed everyone aside and took it upon himself to remove the snake. As the serpent worked its way south toward Kathy Sue's lovely hiney, Weyman shouted, "Don't worry, Kathy Sue. I'll stop it before it tries to make a U-turn!"

Weyman grabbed for the squirming snake, but all he came up with was a handful of Kathy Sue's shapely buttocks. The terrified snake crawled past her step-ins and headed for the apparent security of her ample bosom.

4

Weyman, ever vigilant in his attempt to save the lovely Kathy Sue, reached down the front of her dress in search of the snake. Five minutes later, he snatched the devil from a pit the likes of which it would never find again.

"Are you OK?" Weyman asked Kathy Sue.

"Fine," she answered, smiling at Weyman.

"Are you gonna tell your father what I did?"

"I sure am," said Kathy Sue. "I'm going to tell him you dropped a snake down my dress twice. You do have time, don't you?"

My father, of course, was a super patriot throughout his life, and one of his great pleasures was singing "The Star-Spangled Banner." He was one of the few people who could sing it without bruising the ears of those around him, and he missed no opportunity to bellow it out loud and clear.

Once at a baseball game we attended together, he sang so loudly that everyone around turned and stared. When we sat down, I said, "Daddy, it embarrasses me when you sing the national anthem that loud."

"Son," he replied, "it embarrasses me when you don't."

Years later someone came up with a term that described the sort of heroism I had come to revere. They called it True Grit, and they made a movie by the same name starring John Wayne, "The Duke," who dramatized it as well as anybody could. It was a great movie, a classic, an "outside movie."

Maybe that needs some explanation. You see, there are inside movies and outside movies. An inside movie is where most of the scenes take place inside a house, and there are a lot of women in the cast and a lot of lovey-dovey talk.

Or, worst of all, an inside movie could be an English movie. Every English movie I ever saw had all the "action" take place in a library with a group of people, dressed for dinner, jabbering nonsensically about whether Mrs. Witherington-Kent had done in Mr. Witherington-Kent with poisoned kidney pie.

Outside movies, on the other hand, always involve guns and horses or tanks and planes, and there are a minimum of women. If the hero wants a kiss, he can kiss his horse or tank.

The problem with women in outside movies is that they're always turning their ankles. Hero is trying to get out of a tight spot, and he's dragging Sweet Thing behind him, and suddenly she turns her ankle. So now he's got to pick her up and carry her.

I was watching an outside movie once with Weyman C. Wannamaker, Jr. Alan Ladd was the star, and his horse was dead, he was out of water and he was trying to get through the desert with this dancehall dolly who was tagging along behind him. Sure enough, she turned her ankle.

"What am I going to do with you now?" asked Alan Ladd.

"Leave her for the buzzards!" Weyman screamed from the audience.

Alan Ladd, gentleman that he was, picked up the girl and carried her all the way back to town. Weyman never went to see another Alan Ladd movie. *True Grit*, on the other hand, he saw forty-seven times. Now, that was the quintessential outside movie.

John Wayne played Marshall Rooster Cogburn, a one-eyed, whiskey-swilling, foul-mouthed old coot who goes riding off into Indian territory with Mattie Ross (Kim Darby) and a Texas Ranger named Le Boeuf (Glen Campbell) to find the galoot (Jeff Corey) who shot Mattie's dad and who is also a member of a gang led by the notorious Lucky Ned Pepper (Robert Duvall).

Young Mattie, an expert on human character, picks Rooster Cogburn to lead this mission because she believes he has "true grit." Or, as he is described by another member of the cast, "He's the big fella with the eye patch, and fear don't ever enter his mind."

What eventually happens is that Rooster Cogburn tracks down the varmint who killed Mattie's pa, and then he faces the entire Lucky Ned Pepper gang in a four-against-one shootout.

What a scene! What grit!

Rooster Cogburn advises Ned Pepper that he's taking him in, and Ned Pepper says that's big talk for a one-eyed fat man. So Rooster puts the reins to his horse between his teeth, cocks his rifle with his right hand and draws his pistol with his left and says, "Fill your hands, you son of a bitch!" Then Rooster charges straight ahead even though he's bad outnumbered.

Horse galloping. Hat swept back by the wind. His guns blazing, their guns blazing. Three members of the gang go down and Ned Pepper is filled with holes, but he still has the strength to fire a shot at Rooster, killing his horse.

The horse falls on one of Rooster's legs and traps him. Here comes Lucky Ned aiming to finish him off, but before he can pull the trigger, Glen Campbell picks him off and The Duke escapes another tight spot.

True Grit. John Wayne had it, all right. But so do a lot of other people of far less fame. Folks who have overcome overwhelming odds, have fought and won and fought and lost, have spit in the devil's eye, have soared with eagles despite being surrounded by turkeys, have kissed innumerable frogs in search of a prince, have been bloodied and bullied and tricked and tangled and peed on and pissed off. They're out there everywhere, these unsung heroes. None has ever wiped out an entire gang of outlaws like Rooster Cogburn did, but in their own ways they have robed themselves in The Duke's heroic garb for a moment or two.

There was the morning I drove into Tellico Plains, Tennessee, and walked into a beer joint. I asked the barmaid where I could get breakfast. She said for two dollars she would go to the grocery store and buy the fixings and cook me up something in the back.

It would have been a bargain at any price. Fried eggs. Bacon. Potatoes. I paid her the two dollars for breakfast and then handed her a two dollar tip. She smiled a toothless smile and said, "God bless you, young'un. I been savin' six months and I was just two dollars short."

"Of what?" I asked.

"Of enough to buy me some store-bought teeth," she said. "I ain't chewed nothin' in fifteen years."

I have walked the streets of Yellville, Arkansas, nodding at strangers; I have bought fresh corn from a farmwife in Lodi, Wisconsin; and I have drunk beer with a one-armed man in a beer joint in a town I can't remember somewhere in Oklahoma. I had one too many and asked him where he lost his arm. He said he couldn't remember for sure, but he was certain it would turn up any day now.

I even proposed marriage once on the road. I ate the best fried chicken on earth in the Foley Cafe and Bakery in Foley, Alabama, and I sent the waitress back to tell the woman who cooked that chicken that I would marry her on the spot.

"Doris is already married," said the waitress, "but I ain't." I wiped the grease off my hands and left Foley, Alabama, behind me as quickly as possible.

These are the people I have come to honor. Not those who bask in the spotlight, but the strong, the swift, the courageous who huddle among the masses. True grit comes in many different shapes and sizes, and it often turns up where you least expect to find it.

— 2 —

Profiles in True Grit

A Free Spirit On the Road

I MET AL BERGMAN completely by chance. I was driving through one of Atlanta's spiffiest neighborhoods when I noticed a police car pulled off to the side of the street, blue lights flashing. The policeman was talking to a bearded man of advancing years who appeared to have made a camp in a wooded area just off the street. I figured the policeman was running him in for vagrancy.

"I stopped to investigate a wreck and saw him," the policeman said. "I told him some of the ladies in this neighborhood might complain about him, and that he'd be better off on down the street near the park."

I walked over and introduced myself. His beard was long and full and white. He was sitting next to what appeared to be an old-fashioned wagon. His dog, a German shepherd named Jamie who was tied to a nearby tree, was finishing her supper.

Al Bergman told me he was sixty-nine and that he had retired from the real estate business in Nashville. What he was doing was walking around the United States, pulling the wagon that held his supplies.

"Been thinking about doing something like this for a long time," he said.

Got any family?

"Wife, three kids and nine grandchildren."

And what does the wife think of this odyssey?

"Let's just say it wasn't a joint decision," he answered.

Al Bergman volunteered more information about himself. Said he didn't smoke and that he had jogged for years, which was how he was able to pull his wagon. "I make fifteen miles a day on flat land and about ten when it's hilly." He said he had parachuted into Greece with the OSS during World War II, and that he had been a roadbuilder in South America and later in Vietnam.

I asked if he was afraid camping all alone.

"Jamie's a trained attack dog," he said. "And they taught us how to handle situations in the OSS. I still know how to put a piece of wire around a man's neck.

"Tell you the truth, though, I haven't had one minute's trouble. There are an awful many good people left in this country. They've offered me money and food for me and Jamie, and some of 'em want me to spend the night in their houses. But I don't want to take a thing. I want to do this all by myself."

Al said he was going south out of Atlanta and when he reached the Florida Keys, he would head back up the west coast of Florida, continue along the Gulf and on to California.

"Got to see this country one more time before I'm gone," he said. "And I want to see it the right way — from the ground at one mile an hour."

I asked Al if he were going to heed the policeman's advice and move on down the road to the park.

"No," he said. "I could make it, but I think Jamie's too tired to walk another step."

WEARING HER STORY ON HER BACK

It wasn't the sort of place I would want my mother to catch me in, but there were a few more stories to tell and we didn't want to give up the night quite yet. That's how we ended up in the strip joint.

It didn't take long to figure out the hustle. After each girl danced, she would pick out a table and join those assembled, asking to be bought a drink, which probably was nothing more than Kool-Aid but cost a cool four bucks.

"Hi, I'm Mikki," she said. "Buy me a drink?" She was blonde and young and, judging from her performance on stage, quite athletic. As she sat at our table, I noticed the tattoo on her back.

"It's a horse with wings," she said. "Me and my first husband had 'em done at the same time. He had an American flag done on his back. He was real sexy when he took his shirt off."

For four bucks I figured I might as well get the entire story, so I asked what had happened to her first husband.

"He got blowed up in a factory," she said. "Him and a lot of others. We didn't have no insurance on him, so he left me broke."

"And that's when you started stri — , I mean, dancing?"

"I got married again after that. To a soldier. But he run off."

"So then you started dancing."

"I saw an ad in the paper. I auditioned and got the job. It beats waitin' tables."

"You don't mind dancing in front of all these people without your clothes on?"

"Don't bother me. The more that watches, the more tips I get. I made $200 last weekend."

It was an orderly process: While the girls danced, the men slipped bills under garters worn at the thigh. After their routines, the dancers rewarded the tippers with a kiss.

Mikki said she wasn't going to stay in town much longer, that she was heading to Las Vegas to be a chorus girl. "I hear they make two thousand a week out there," she said.

"And you won't have to kiss anybody for tips," I added.

"Kissin' don't bother me," she said. "Kiss enough frogs and you might find a prince."

She put down her glass, winked and went back to dance and kiss again. I wondered if she would ever make it to Vegas. I wondered if she would ever find a prince. I doubted it, but tattooed strippers have a right to dream, too.

SAYING AN AGE-OLD GOODBYE

There were maybe half a hundred of us in the airport concourse waiting for the call to board. Some read. Some stared. Some stumbled through awkward goodbyes.

Jets have taken away some of the romance of saying goodbye. When you said goodbye at a train station, there were tears and long last kisses. Saying goodbye at an airport, I thought, is like leaving to go to a convenience store for a box of cereal.

Then I saw the kid and his mother. She had to be his mother. The kid was a Marine but obviously hadn't been one for long. His uniform was ill-fitting and seemed to itch. He had some hair but not much.

The kid was leaving on the plane. His mother had come to say goodbye. I let my imagination run at its own pace.

He looked nineteen, tops. She was in her late thirties or early forties, still a pretty woman. She never took her eyes off him, trying, I suspect, to memorize every detail of him so that when she missed him, which would be every day, she could recall his face and maybe ease the pain a little.

He seemed terribly uncomfortable. I guessed him to have boot camp behind him. He had been home on leave. Now he was being sent to his first assignment — adult sort of stuff. The last thing he needed was a doting mother who wouldn't take her eyes off him at the airport.

He smoked a cigarette as they talked. Or, as his mother talked. He only nodded, or grunted, or gave an occasional yes or no and then took another pull off his cigarette. He was new at cigarettes, too. He tried to flick the ashes off with a finger but flicked the fire instead. The hot ashes landed on the jacket of his uniform.

His mother quickly brushed off the fire before there was any damage to the government-issued fabric. That embarrassed the kid, too. A Marine doesn't flick the fire from his cigarette onto the jacket of his uniform, and even if he does, his mother doesn't brush it away.

I wondered about the kid's father, the mother's husband. Why hadn't he come? He was probably dead. No. He had probably split, and that's why the mother hovered about her son so and wished that he didn't have to leave her and dreaded the loneliness that surely would follow.

Their time ran out.

"When do you think you'll be back?" the mother asked.

"Christmas, I guess," the kid answered.

"It's a long time to Christmas," she said.

"Yeah," grunted the kid.

"You'll write me?"

"I'll write you."

"Be careful."

"OK."

"I love you," she said.

The kid mumbled back all that would come out. His mother kissed him. He let her, and then he disappeared down the walkway to the plane.

She wiped something from the corner of her eye and went home to wait for Christmas.

A MEMORY GOOD FOR A LIFETIME

We had only one real Christmas together, my mother, my father and I. Only one Christmas when we were actually in our own house with a tree, with coffee and cake left out for Santa, with an excited five-year-old awakening to a pair of plastic cowboy pistols, a straw cowboy hat and an autographed picture of Hopalong Cassidy.

My first Christmas I was only a couple of months old; that doesn't count. Then we were traveling around for a couple of years. The Army does that to you. Then there was Korea. And then we had that one Christmas together before whatever demons my father brought back from Korea sent him to roaming for good.

That one and only Christmas together, my father had duty until noon on Christmas eve. I waited for him at the screen door, sitting and staring until that blue Hudson, "The Blue Goose" as my father called it, pulled into the driveway. I ran out and jumped into his arms.

"Ready for Santa?" he asked.

"I've been ready since August," I shouted.

But before we could settle in for our Christmas, my father had to take care of a problem. He had found this family — the old man out of work, in need of a shave and a haircut, and his wife crying because her babies were hungry. My father, whatever else he was, was a giving man. He couldn't stand to have when others didn't.

"They're flat on their butts and it's Christmas," I remember his saying to my mother. "Nobody deserves that."

So he somehow found a barber willing to leave home on Christmas eve, and he took the old man in for a shave and a haircut. Then he bought the family groceries. Sacks and sacks of groceries. He bought toys for the kids, of which there was a house full. The poor are often fruitful.

We didn't leave them until dusk. The old man and the woman thanked us, and the kids watched us with wondering eyes. As we drove away in "The Blue Goose," my father broke down and cried. My mother cried, too. I cried because they were crying.

We all slept together that night and cried ourselves to sleep. Next morning, I had my pistols and my hat and my picture of Hopalong Cassidy.

Maybe the three of us had only one real Christmas together — my father had left by the time the next one rolled around — but it was a Christmas a man can carry around for a lifetime. Each year at Christmas, with my father long since in his grave, I thank God that one is mine to remember.

GETTING WHAT HE DESERVED

There were seven or eight of us in line, waiting to pay the cashier for our lunches. We were all in a hurry because that's the way of the American business-day lunch. At the front of the line was a woman with a small boy of about eight. He was a cute little fellow wearing jeans, sneakers and a pullover sweater. A shock of dark hair fell over his eyes.

As the woman fumbled in her purse, looking for money to pay her check, the kid noticed a display of candy bars beside the cash register and immediately wanted one.

"You can't have any candy," said his mother. "You had pie with your lunch."

"But I want some candy," said the kid. His tone was surprisingly insistent. Almost belligerent.

The mother continued her search for money in her purse, and the kid continued to whine about the candy. Then he began to stomp his foot.

The rest of us in line were beginning to get restless. We bunched a little closer together and several folks began mumbling under their breath.

"Ought to snatch him bald," said one man quietly.

The kid by now was reaching for the candy display in open opposition to his mother. She grabbed his arm and pulled it away, but not before he clutched a Snickers bar in his hand.

"Put that back!" said his mother.

"No!" shouted the child, his lips pooched out in a classic pout. It was an arrogant "No!" A why-don't-you-try-and-make-me "No!"

The line bunched even more closely together, and the man who had suggested snatching the kid bald appeared ready to do so himself. So much for the kid's shock of dark hair, I thought.

But the mother moved suddenly and with purpose. She paid the cashier, took back her change and dropped it into her purse. Then with one quick motion, she grabbed hold of the child's pullover sweater and lifted him off the floor. The moment his sneakers came back to earth, she turned his back toward her and began flailing his backside. She flailed and flailed. A look of disbelief came across the kid's face. His eyes filled with tears. He tried to break away, but that incensed his mother more, and she flailed him again.

When she had finished administering the punishment, she turned the child around and pointed a finger squarely in his sobbing face. With a voice strong and certain, she said, "The next time I tell you to do something, young man, will you do it?"

The child looked at the floor. Meekly and sincerely, he replied, "Yes, ma'am."

The mother turned to go. The child returned the Snickers bar without further hesitation and marched dutifully out behind her.

The rest of us in line broke into spontaneous applause.

A NOBLEMAN IN RAGS

Alvin was a thirty-year-old black man. He was one of the street people in our nation's capital, Washington, D.C. He had no job. No money. He slept and ate in shelters for the poor. He told horror stories about some of the folks in those shelters.

I met Alvin on a cold, fall day as we both stood in Lafayette Park across from the White House. Within sight of that great edifice and all it represents, I was a soft touch when he asked me for a handout. As I gave him a dollar, I asked how he got in the shape he was in.

"I'm from Dayton, Ohio," he answered freely. "I moved to Maryland with this woman who was in the Navy. One night I came home drunk and she started hittin' on me.

Look here at this knot on my arm. That's where she got me with a stick.

"I was drunk and I got mad and whipped her ass. The police came and got me, and I was in jail for two months. When I got out, my woman had moved off with another man. I still miss that woman. Especially at night," he said.

"I came here to look for a job, but there ain't no jobs. I had nearly 'bout a thousand dollars when I got here, but that ran out pretty fast and I started sleeping in them shelters. I called my mama in Dayton and told her a lie, and she sent me fifty dollars. She thinks I'm doin' good here, and I don't want to break her heart and tell her I been in jail."

Alvin apparently had been drinking again. When he talked about his mother, tears welled in his eyes.

"I'm gonna stay here until I get me a construction job or something like that. I ain't never gonna let my mama see me like this."

There was no way to listen to his story in the shadow of the White House and fail to see the shocking contrast between the two Americas — the one within and the one without. Across the street, Ron and Nancy and the king of Saudi Arabia, drinking champagne and eating caviar. In Lafayette Park, Alvin in his rags, begging for a handout.

I asked him if he was angry with Ronald Reagan, who is supposed to be heartless when it comes to the poor.

"He ain't the one that got drunk and beat up his woman and got throwed in jail. That was me," Alvin said. "I got myself into this mess, and I got to get myself out of it now."

I think I said something stupid like, "Well, hang in there," but forgive me. It's not every day that I'm confronted with nobility in rags.

***

Al Bergman, the sixty-nine-year-old free spirit on the road

with his dog Jamie, looking for peace and the soul of America. Mikki the stripper, a third his age but already in search of the same dream. One mother sending her Marine son off to the real world, far from her protective bosom; another trying to teach her young son discipline. And Alvin, down on his luck but not on himself or his country.

In their own ways, each of these people is an embodiment of true grit. You can hear it in their voices, see it in their eyes, feel it in their stories. It's there just as surely as it was when Marshall Rooster Cogburn took those reins between his teeth and rode out to face Lucky Ned Pepper and his gang. And yet as real as it is, it seems indefinable.

What is true grit? Where does it come from? How did it get there? These are the questions books are made of.

— 3 —

Never Go Camping With A Man Who Drinks Whiskey Sours

ONE OF THE THINGS John Wayne had going for him in *True Grit* (and in real life, for that matter) was that he looked the part. Tall, strong, ruggedly handsome and tough to the bone. The way he walked, the way he talked, the clothes he wore — all these things added to his aura.

The same was true of another of my childhood heroes, Superman. When he was dressed as Clark Kent, mild-mannered reporter for a large metropolitan newspaper — black-rimmed glasses, white shirt, striped tie, blue suit and wing-tipped shoes — nobody paid him any attention. Certainly not Lois Lane. But the minute he switched into that tight-fitting Superman costume and started leaping tall buildings in a single bound, Lois was on him like bark on a tree.

So maybe "the look" is part of the recipe for true grit. I'm not arguing that clothes make the man, but I've dated enough women hiding vast quantities of themselves under muumuus to know that diversionary tactics can work.

It's easy enough to chronicle the traditional manly characteristics which The Duke embodied. For one, he always seemed to have a couple of days worth of stubble on his chin and a little hair hanging over his collar.

I have more than a couple of days worth of stubble; I've got a beard. I decided to grow it several years ago after someone called me "fishface." I think the implication was that I have a weak chin. I found that a beard made me look more mature and even gave me an air of pseudo-sophistication. I liked it.

So I took the look one step further and started smoking cigars. They, too, I reasoned, made me look mature and urbane. One day while smoking my cigar, I accidentally knocked the fire off the end. I didn't immediately see where it fell, but I soon discovered that a burning beard gives off a terrible odor.

I gave up cigars after that frightening experience and started carrying a copy of the *Wall Street Journal* under my arm. It gave me the same aura of authority and, whereas a cigar lasts no more than an hour or so, I could carry the same *Wall Street Journal* around for a week or more before it started turning yellow and I had to buy another.

Anyway, I have the beard, and I also have the hair over the collar. In fact, I've been wearing my hair long for years. It's like a muumuu for my ears.

I never noticed that I had big ears until I was in the fourth grade and Alvin Bates pointed them out to me. "Your ears poke way out," he said. I looked in a mirror and discovered that for once in his life he wasn't lying. I also had a lot of freckles on my nose, and when I smiled I bore an amazing resemblance to Howdy Doody, the late puppet. I hoped that no one else noticed the similarity.

"How's Clarabell?" asked Alvin Bates in a loud voice the next morning when I walked into class. That was only the beginning of the abuse I took from my classmates.

"Mind putting your head down on your desk?" the girl who sat behind me asked one day during an arithmetic lesson.

I didn't have any better sense at the time than to ask her why.

"Because, Howdy," she said to the delight of the jackals sitting around her, "I can't see the blackboard for your ears."

I tried everything to make my ears grow closer to my head. At night I slept with a rubber band around my head to hold my ears in. Can you imagine how much it hurt when the rubber band broke in the middle of the night? I even tried gluing my ears to my head. Inevitably one of them would come unglued, leaving me looking like I was giving signals to a train.

My only salvation came years later when long hair, fashionably trimmed over the ears, came into style. But even that caused me some trauma.

You will remember that my father was a military man and consequently was not fond of long hair. Many times his cohorts told me the story of how he dealt with a young recruit sporting more than regulation locks:

"We had some new recruits come in to Fort Benning," the story began, "and they sent the Captain, your old man, out to look them over and get them checked out for their first day on post. He came to this little ol' skinny boy with hair down over his eyes and way down on the bottom of his neck. That wouldn't be anything today, but back then he looked real strange.

"Your daddy looked him up and down real slow and then

made a horrible face and said, 'Son, as soon as I dismiss you, I want you to go over to the hospital and check yourself in. Have the doctors give you a thorough going over.'

"The kid said to your daddy, 'Do you think there's something wrong with me, sir?'

"Your daddy said, 'Yes, indeed, soldier. I think beyond a shadow of a doubt that if the doctors look close enough, somewhere on you they will find a vagina.'"

Even after all these years, I can handle the guilt better than my uncovered ears.

***

Another thing common to men like Rooster Cogburn is that they're bad to drink or chew or do both. You can tell a lot about people by noticing what they drink. For instance, I was in a restaurant recently when a man walked in and asked the hostess, "How long before I can have a table?"

"About fifteen minutes," the hostess said.

"Good," the man answered. "That'll give me time for a whiskey sour at the bar."

I can't explain why, but a whiskey sour is a drink for a man whose mother made him practice piano a lot when he was a kid. A man who drinks whiskey sours also probably throws a baseball like a girl — limp wristed. A man who drinks whiskey sours and then eats that silly little cherry they put in the bottom probably has a cat or a poodle for a pet. In other words, I wouldn't go on a camping trip with a man who drinks whiskey sours.

Scotch drinkers are aggressive. They order like they're Charles Bronson trying to have a quick shot before returning to the subway to kill a few punks and thugs.

"What'll you have, sir?" asks the bartender.

"Cutty. Water. Rocks. Twist," growls the Scotch drinker. I think maybe Scotch drinkers wear their underwear too tight.

You have to watch people who drink vodka or gin. "Anybody who drinks see-through whiskey," an old philosopher once said, "will get crazy." Indeed. Vodka and gin drinkers are the type who leave the house to get a loaf of bread, drop by the bar for just one, and return home six weeks later. With the bread.

I wouldn't go on a camping trip with anyone who drinks vodka or gin, either. They're the types who would invite snakes, raccoons and bears over for cocktails and then wind up getting into an argument about tree frogs.

Bourbon drinkers never grow up. Eight out of ten started drinking bourbon with Coke in school and still have a pair of saddle oxfords in the closet. Bourbon drinkers don't think they've had a good time unless they get sick and pass out under a coffee table.

Then there are the white wine drinkers. Never get involved in any way with them. They either want to get married, sell you a piece of real estate or redecorate your house.

As for myself, I'm a beer drinker. We're usually honest, straightforward people. We also are usually kind and quite sentimental and will get cryin'-about-our-daddies drunk with one another. That's just before we destroy the establishment in which we're drinking because somebody made an offhand remark about Richard Petty or the memory of Patsy Cline.

Never go camping with a beer drinker, either. We're really no fun unless there's a jukebox around, and we belch a lot, which might frighten the snakes, raccoons, bears and tree frogs.

I occasionally get an urge to chew tobacco, and snuff-dipping is a part of my heritage, but I have a distinct problem with both. I'm talking about the mess they make.

There used to be two popular commercials promoting snuff, one featuring former professional football player Walt ("Just a pench between yo' cheek and gum") Garrison and another starring famous fiddle player and singer Charlie Daniels. The commercials always showed these fellows smiling as they snuffed up, but they never showed them spitting. If you dip, you spit. If you dip and don't spit, your have swallowed your snuff and soon will die a slow, agonizing death unless somebody has a stomach pump handy.

My grandmother was a snuff user. She used to send me to the store to buy her "medicine," as she called it. Then she would sit for hours with her Bible in her lap and a dip behind her lip. I knew it wasn't medicine. If it had been, no one would have kept it in their mouth that long.

One afternoon while returning from the store with my grandmother's "medicine," I decided to sample it. The convulsions began immediately. I managed to spit some of it out, but most of it went in my nose and eyes. The remaining portion I swallowed. If there had been a doctor nearby, I would have been pronounced dead on arrival at home. Month-old lettuce looked better than I did.

If there were truth in advertising, manufacturers of snuff would be required to print a warning on the side of the cans: "Dip or chew if you want, but know that you're going to have to spit every eight seconds or so and probably will get it all over your shoes."

Not only do those snuff commercials fail to show people spitting, they also never show them with spittle curling out of the corners of their mouths. "Dip or chew if you want," another warning should say, "but be prepared to look like you've been eating mud."

I have a friend who has been chewing tobacco for years. Like all other chewers, he spits a lot and juice runs out the sides of his mouth. His wife tried to get him to stop because she was offended by the little spit cups she found all over the house. There's nothing more unappealing than a cup of day-old tobacco spit.

Finally she said to him, "That's it. I've had it. Either the chewing tobacco goes or I go."

"Honey," my friend replied, "I don't have but one vice. I don't stay out drunk, I don't chase women and I'm kind to children, old people and dogs. But my daddy chewed and his daddy before him, and chewing is in my blood. Asking me to give it up is like asking a dog to stop licking his privates. I couldn't stop even if I wanted to."

His wife studied on his statement for a few moments and said, "OK, if it means that much to you, I suppose I can live with it."

Soon afterwards they were celebrating their wedding anniversary. My friend's wife gave him a leather pouch for storing his chewing tobacco and he gave her the promise that he'd go outside whenever he needed to spit.

That compromise took guts on both their parts — so much, in fact, that I was inspired to write a poem about it. It went like this:

True love.
True grit.
You need 'em both
When you've got to spit.
Ptui.

***

Another ingredient of true grit, judging from most of The Duke's movies, could be body odor. Think about it: Except for when he wrestled some galoot into the river and knocked him senseless, did you ever see that pilgrim bathe? No, sir. The Duke liked to smell like a man . . .or at least like a man who had been riding the range for a month without a bath.

Back before air conditioning became one of the elements essential to life, it was perfectly all right to sweat a little and to emit an aromatic scent. Everybody did. Your mother sweated over a hot stove. Your father sweated at work and then came home and sat around in his underwear and sweated some more. At the end of a long day, nobody asked, "Where did you park your goats?" Nobody said, "Isn't it about time you looked for a reliable underarm deodorant?"

Today, sweat stains under the arms are considered only slightly less offensive than Joan Rivers. They can lead to the loss of a big account: "Sorry, Wilson, but we're going to have to find ourselves a new boy. Those perspiration stains on your shirt are a disgrace to the firm." Or to the loss of a lover: "I'll always love you, Marvin, but you've got the Okefenokee Swamp under your arms." Or even to the breakup of a family: "I'm filing for divorce, Donna. Those underarm stains on your tennis blouse are ruining the children's chances at a full and happy life."

Mandatory air conditioning not only did away with underarm sweat stains, it also led to the demise of a great tradition: the paddle fan. In the little Methodist church in my hometown, there were always Cokesbury hymnals and paddle fans along the back of each pew. The fans generally were provided by either a funeral home or an ambitious politician, with their message on one side — "Arnold's Funeral Home/Free Parking" or "Vote for Grover (Shorty) Turnipseed, County Commissioner" — and a four-color biblical scene on the other side (usually the Last Supper).

It wasn't necessary to listen to the minister's words to know whether or not he was reaching back for one of those you-had-better-change-your-evil-ways sermons. All you had to do was watch the congregation. The faster they fanned themselves, the closer to home the preacher was hitting.

The mere mention of the evils of alcohol was certain to speed the fanning strokes, and when the minister began to describe the warm climate that one who imbibed could expect at his final address, a draft no manner of air conditioner could match would roar through the sanctuary off those paper fans.

If I were a minister today, I would use a two-prong attack to challenge my backsliding flock. First, I would turn off the air conditioning some hot Sunday morning, and then I would explain the major difference between the two possible destinations that awaited them: hell for companionship, perhaps; heaven for its climate. Then I would quietly take my seat and let them sweat out their decisions without benefit of paddle fans. Now, that's the sort of situation that develops true grit.

Our preoccupation with smelling any way except natural doesn't end with air conditioning and deodorant, of course. "Is your mouthwash doing the job?" asked a commercial on television the other night. I don't know the answer to that. I brush my teeth every day whether they need it or not, and I even gargle on occasion. But how do I know if my mouth has that awful medicine smell they were talking about on TV?

I can hear my friends now: "He's a decent guy, but somebody really ought to tell him he has medicine mouth."

The same is true of shampoo. According to current commercials, if the shampoo you're using doesn't clean your hair, remove all dandruff, and leave your hair bright and shiny and full of body and smelling like a flower shop, people might not allow you in the same room with their children. You could infect the little boogers.

The new shampoos, of course, are highly scented, and one even leaves your hair smelling like apricots. Here's a hint: If you happen to be a man, never walk into a truck stop with your hair smelling like apricots. Someone likely will make fruit salad out of your head.

Come to think of it, that's probably the kind of shampoo that Lucky Ned Pepper was using, and that's why the marshall was so riled. That and the fact that just before their big shootout, Ned yelled across to Rooster Cogburn, "Hey, big guy, what's your sign?"

***

Another quality I associate with The Duke is that he was always friendly with his critters. His horse loved him. His cattle loved him. And in several movies he had a dog by his side. A man needs a good dog — one who'll fetch a stick and lick his hand. Don't forget what Bullet did for Roy Rogers and what Rin Tin Tin did for Sergeant Preston.

I'm not talking about those highfaluting purebreds who have been pampered by their owners and registered with the American Kennel Club. I don't like pampered children, and I don't like pampered dogs. I want a dog with character and personality, one who had to turn over a trash can once in a while just to keep food in his stomach. And I like a dog who knows enough about where puppies come from that he can choose his own mate and take care of business without waiting for some high-hatted human to "arrange" a canine tête-à-tête for him.

Allow me to explain the types of dogs that I like and probably the kind The Duke liked, too:

● YARD DOGS — A yard dog, usually found in the rural South, is a likable sort who hangs around the back door waiting for table scraps and who crawls under trucks to get in the shade on hot days. Yard dogs are recognizable by the oil and grease on their backs and by the humble way they walk sideways toward the individual calling them.

• HOG DOGS — These are fat little dogs who come from a union of Lord-knows-what and will eat anything that is put before them. They will lick the pan clean and beg for more. In rare cases, these dogs have been know to suck eggs. On the positive side of the ledger, such dogs make the expense of a garbage disposal unnecessary.

• LAP DOGS — These are very loving dogs who crave attention and leap onto your lap and lick your face and shed all over the sofa. They especially enjoy lying on their backs and kicking their legs back and forth while you scratch their bellies. I had a great lap dog once. My wife used to scratch the dog's belly for hours. When I asked her to do the same for me, she called her mother and told her I was perverted.

• A.J. FOYT DOGS — These dogs enjoy standing on the side of the road and racing with cars when they drive by. Every neighborhood has at least one. The problem with such dogs is that they tend to become frustrated after never being able to outrun passing cars, so they resort to gnawing the tires on your car when it's parked in the driveway. They also tend to have short life spans, because sooner or later they catch one of those cars.

• SHOE DOGS — These are dogs with a shoe fetish. Leave a pair of shoes out one night and by morning they'll have them chewed back to the raw material stage. Never take a shoe dog into a Gucci store; you could be bankrupt within minutes. Regional variations of this dog will chew eyeglasses, leather-bound books, remote control devices and Tupperware.

***

Finally, one of The Duke's most obvious characteristics, and an essential element, it seems to me, of true grit, was his self-sufficiency. He didn't need nobody for nothing.

I've always tried to emulate John Wayne in that regard. I've tried to learn to feed myself, clothe myself and fix leaky pipes. After all, you never know when your wife may leave and take your dog with her.

The first thing a breathing, self-sufficient male has to learn to do is feed himself. I'm not talking about eating out or ordering pizza. There was a time when I ordered out for pizza so many times that the delivery boy started getting phone calls and his mail at my house. But that's cheating; self-sufficiency means doing it yourself.

So, armed with determination and an unused kitchen in a new house, I set out to cook for myself. The first thing I did was buy one of those amazing food processors. "This food processor is the state of the art," said the saleslady. "You can make your own mayonnaise with it."

Why would anybody want to make their own mayonnaise, I wondered, when the Hellman's people are perfectly willing to do it for them? Self-sufficiency, I answered.

The next morning I decided to make myself a hearty omelette. I had never made one before, but I knew I needed at least eggs, onions, tomatoes, ham and cheese. First I decided to chop the onion in my new food processor. In less than ten seconds, I had a food processor full of onion juice. I have no idea what happened to the onion itself.

I immediately deleted onions from the recipe and proceeded. Next I put a piece of uncooked ham in my microwave oven and set the dial for five minutes. When I returned with the morning paper under my arm, the ham looked like Sherman had passed through Atlanta again. I mean, to a crisp.

Not to worry. Ham is high in cholesterol and unnecessary for a good omelette anyway. Remembering my experience with the onion and the food processor, I decided to slice the tomato by hand. Meanwhile, I put the cheese in the microwave to soften it.

When I had stopped the bleeding on my first two fingers, I checked the cheese in the microwave. That afternoon, it took the Roto-Rooter man only forty minutes to get the cheese unstuck from the sides of the oven.

I judiciously decided to forget about the omelette and simply have scrambled eggs with fresh orange juice. If the food processor would turn a fresh onion into onion juice, I reasoned it would do the same thing to an orange. I was correct. In seconds I had fresh orange juice. It tasted terrible, however. I later figured that maybe I should have peeled the orange.

I still had the eggs. The part that didn't stick to the bottom of the pan tasted like Silly Putty, so I threw the entire mess into my new garbage disposal which promptly clogged.

I waited until the pizza place opened and ordered a medium with everything except anchovies. It came with anchovies anyway, so I scraped them off the top of my pizza and electrocuted them in my microwave oven. I felt momentarily vindicated — after all, the microwave did what I intended it to do — but I felt far from self-sufficient.

That evening while watching television, I saw a commercial for a book that promised to save me hundreds of dollars a year in home repair and improvement bills. If I ordered one of these books, the announcer said, I would be able to fix my plumbing and even build myself a new patio.

No I wouldn't. I don't care how many of those books I read, I can't build or repair anything. A hammer is high technology to me.

When I was a kid, my mother bought me an erector set. I

read the instructions and tried to build a crane. "Oh, look," my mother exclaimed when I finished. "You've built a 1948 DeSoto with both doors missing."

I was so inept they wouldn't allow me to play with the garden hose. "Get away from that hose," my mother would say. "You know you don't know nothing about machinery."

I carried this lack of knowledge into high school, where I enrolled in shop class in an effort to improve myself. As my term project, I decided to build a chair.

"What is it?" asked the shop teacher at the end of the quarter.

"It's a chair," I said.

"Looks more like a wooden model of a 1948 DeSoto with both doors missing to me," he said.

As an adult, I've always had the same problem, particularly with automobiles. "What seems to be the problem with your car?" the auto mechanic asks me.

"It's broken," I answer.

He opens the hood and looks inside at all that infernal wiring and all those other doflatchies and what's-its that make a car run. "Here's your problem," he says. "Your lola-bridgelator isn't gee-hawing with your double-low, E-flat commodgelator."

What does that mean? And how did he learn that?

Around the house I'm equally confused. When I moved into a new house and tried to take a shower, there was no hot water. I called the plumber. "Here's your problem," he said. "The letters on your shower knobs are wrong. The 'H' is on the cold knob and the 'C' is on the hot knob."

It cost me nearly $200 to have the plumber move the knobs on my pipes so I would have hot water when I turned the "H" knob.

I did think I could at least build a stand for my mailbox at the new house. I went out and bought lumber and nails and bolts. I now have the only mailbox stand in town that looks like a 1948 DeSoto with the doors missing.

Finally I did find one thing mechanical that I could fix when it broke. I can stop a commode from making that annoying sound it makes sometimes after you flush it. What you do is lift the lid off the top of the commode and fiddle with the rubber dohickey until the sound stops.

Try finding that kind of information in a stupid book.

My last attempt at self-sufficiency almost proved fatal. I had a bad case of the flu, but I resolved to lick it myself without running to the doctor to have him laugh at me. Real men stick it out.

I felt worse than a five-eyed goat in a sandstorm. I was so sick my toenails turned black. I couldn't breathe, I couldn't eat and my tongue itched. I turned to would-be friends for help and advice.

"Here's what you do," one said confidently. "You pour a glass full of bourbon and then you take a tablespoon of sugar. You eat the sugar and chase it with the glass of bourbon and then go to bed. You'll feel great the next morning."

He was partially right. I felt great while I was in the coma caused by the sugar and bourbon. When I came out of it, however, I felt just as bad as I did before.

Somebody else told me to eat lots of mustard. "It's an old custom in my family. A cup of mustard a day will cure anything."

Anything, that is, except the flu. Eating a cup of mustard without hot dogs will make your ears water.

The next advice I got was to eat honey and chase it with a heavy dose of castor oil. "Honey and castor oil will purify you and cleanse all the poison from your body," I was told.

Maybe so, but eating honey and chasing it with a heavy-duty dose of castor oil also will keep you from sitting in one place for more than five minutes for days. Captured enemy spies were threatened with the same treatment during World War II by Allied interrogators. It always worked.

Still another friend suggested that an afternoon in a sauna would be just the thing to put me back in the pink. "You get into a sauna for about an hour," said the friend, "and then you come out and drink a strong vodka tonic. Go back into the sauna for another hour and then come out and drink two vodka tonics. You return to the sauna for a third hour, then come out and finish off the bottle of vodka."

"Sounds great," I said. "A sauna should really help me."

"You kiddin'? Saunas are awful for a man in your condition, but after a bottle of vodka, who cares?"

Chicken soup was the final suggestion. "Do I put vodka or castor oil in it?" I asked sheepishly.

"No, silly. Chicken soup by itself has tremendous curative powers."

I ate so much chicken soup that I had the urge to go peck corn, but I was still too sick to get off my tail feathers and go outside.

Eventually I cured myself by doing what any real man would do in a similar situation: I pulled the covers up over my head, whined and felt sorry for myself. In a couple of days, I was fine. A victory for self-sufficiency.

***

So is it the stubbly beard, the long hair, drinking and chewing, sweating and stinking, loving dogs and being self-sufficient that gives a person true grit?

There must be more to it than that. Otherwise, how would you explain the likes of Eugene Ellis?

— 4 —

A Heaping
Helping of Grit

Setting A Shining Example

IT USED TO BE that there were a lot of people around —
on street corners, in barber shops, in train stations and
airports — who would shine your shoes for a price. But
shining shoes got to be a social stigma, a sign of subser-
vience in some people's minds, and so shoe shining has
gone the way of service at gas stations: It's there, but you
have to look for it.

When I met Eugene Ellis shining shoes in Macon, Georgia, I asked him if it bothered his self-image that he was still
shining shoes for a living. He answered my question by
looking at me like I was crazy.

Eugene Ellis is sixty-two years old. He's black. He's short,
which he says is helpful when you shine shoes because you
don't have to bend over as far. Eugene Ellis is an orphan, a
husband and a father of five. He shines shoes all day in a
barbershop, and then he shines for a good part of the

evening in a local jazz bar.

He started shining shoes on the streets of Macon when he was five. Years later at the Atlanta airport, he shined the shoes of a young senator who hoped someday to be president of the United States. John Kennedy told Eugene that when he was elected president, he would give him a job shining shoes at the White House.

"Said he'd come back and get me," recalled Eugene, "but I didn't think he would."

Eugene Ellis shined shoes at the White House for three presidents — Kennedy, Lyndon Johnson and Richard Nixon — before he decided it was time to go back home. He brought memories with him:

On Kennedy — "A good Catholic man. Real quiet. I was in the eighth car back when they shot him."

On Johnson — "If he was still president, I'd still be shining his shoes. He always took me to the ranch with him."

On Nixon — "He was a little different from the others."

Eugene shined the shoes of Hubert Humphrey, Gerald Ford, Muhammad Ali, Don McNeal and Elvis Presley. He said Elvis paid the best of the bunch.

The worst shoe to shine? "Patent leather. Can't see what you've done."

Favorite shoe to shine? "Anything in bad shape. I like to see my work when I'm finished with it."

It would be easy to try to attach some social significance to this story and say that what this country needs today is more people shining shoes like Eugene Ellis does, and wouldn't that solve some of the unemployment problem? But "let 'em shine shoes" isn't exactly my style, so I'll just let it pass with this:

Eugene Ellis, who has put three daughters through college, gets salary plus tips at a regular job. And when he pulled out his wallet to show me a card some prince gave him at the White House, it was filled with what he called his "lucky twenties." His work is inside and requires no heavy lifting, it beats scraping dead bugs off windshields, and he says that when he's got a good pair of shoes to shine and his rag is popping just right, "it's like I'm making music."

Yeah, I think that's enough said.

WISDOM IN RETROSPECT

The courtesy van showed up to take me to the airport at Salt Lake City. The driver was a woman, probably in her late thirties. They had been hard years. You can see it in a person's face sometimes.

She asked where I was headed, and I told her Atlanta.

"That's where you live?" she asked.

"Don't I sound like it?" I answered.

She just laughed. "Yeah, you do. I was married to an ol' Georgia boy once."

"Where from?"

"Albany."

There was a story there. "How in the world did someone from way out here in Utah get hooked up with someone from Albany, Georgia?"

"Met him on the bus," she said. "I was just nineteen. Was going to Boise, Idaho, to visit my grandparents. He was in the service on his way to Anchorage, Alaska. He sat down next to me when we left Salt Lake. He was a real quiet boy and shy. Didn't say a word the first hour, but then he started talking a little. I could tell he was homesick.

"He showed me some pictures he had in his wallet. When we got to Boise, he helped me get my bags off the bus and asked if he could write me some time. I said he could. Then one day he wrote and asked if I would marry him. I accepted. I was nineteen and had the moon and the stars in my eyes. We got married and drove all the way to Albany for our honeymoon," she continued.

"We had seven years together and two kids."

"You got divorced?" I pried.

"He was Baptist. I was Mormon. That was one of several things that were wrong. After I split with him I stayed single for seven more years. Then I got to figuring my kids needed a daddy, so I went out and found them one."

"How did that work out?"

"Bad. You can't make a daddy out of just anybody, I found out."

We were getting close to the airport. "You married now?" I asked, hoping for an end to the story.

"I'm living with a fellow now," said my driver. "I guess we moved in together about two years ago. My mother is shocked because we don't go ahead and get married. She says what we're doing is sinful. It might be but we're happy. I guess I'm as happy now as I've ever been. I don't want to take a chance of messing up again. Getting married don't solve any problems, it starts 'em."

As I stepped out of the van, I asked her name.

"It's Dixie."

I didn't have time to find out why. I simply said, "Stay happy, Dixie."

She smiled, nodded and drove away. Somebody in Utah has himself a good woman, I thought to myself. I just hope he knows it.

EXERCISING DISCRETION IN TENNESSEE

My friend Stephens and I were returning from a camping

trip somewhere in the hills of Tennessee when we developed an urgent thirst. He pulled into the first place with beer signs he spotted — a cement-block building with a lot of pickup trucks parked outside.

"Let's go in here," Stephens said.

The first thing I noticed inside was a pool table. Pool can be a dangerous game when played in a church basement. When played in a place like this, customers should be issued hockey helmets.

The crowd gave us the ol' they-ain't-from-around-here look as we moved quietly toward a table. I noticed a sign over the bar which said, "It is a felony to carry a weapon where alcoholic beverages are served." You didn't put a sign like that on your wall, I reasoned, unless there had been a previous incident, or incidents, to warrant it.

I usually can pick out a troublemaker, and there's one in every bar in America. In this instance, he was standing at the counter. He had long sideburns and his cigarettes rolled up in the sleeve of his shirt, a sure sign of a belligerent personality.

The tough guy picked up his beer and walked toward us. I drew a bead on the front door.

"Either of you shoot pool?" he asked.

"No," said Stephens.

"No, sir," I said.

The tough guy just grunted. "Guess I'll have to shoot by myself," he said.

Pool can be a very macho game. A man attacks a pool table, especially on the break when he makes every effort to shatter the balls.

The tough guy knew every eye was on him. He chalked his stick confidently, aimed the blue tip toward the rack of balls, closed one eye and came forward through the cue ball with an enormous grunt. But there was no ear-splitting sound of balls colliding. The tough guy had whiffed the cue ball.

The room fell silent. Nobody dared move a muscle. The tough guy, fighting to keep his cool, lined up the cue ball again as quickly as possible and this time scattered the balls around the table.

Stephens and I finished our beer, paid our tab and drove away.

"How far we been?" I asked him a little later.

"About ten miles," he said.

"Think we're safe?" I asked.

"Nothing out here but the bears and possums," he answered.

Then, and only then, did we allow ourselves the marvelous relief of howling laughter.

THE GIFT OF LOVING A CHILD

"I just want one thing," Sherry said to me. "I want people to learn of the tragedies we have been through so maybe they will understand how important it is to love their children with all their hearts and souls. To love a child is one of God's greatest gifts."

Sherry and D.A. were just kids themselves when they married nearly twenty-one years ago. Their first child was Lex, a boy. Then came another son, Allan.

"After Allan," Sherry explained, "we felt, in this day and time, that two children were enough. I was having some health problems, too, so I agreed to have my tubes tied."

They settled in the small town of Calhoun, Georgia, an hour or so north of Atlanta. Sherry taught elementary school, and D.A. became high school head football coach.

When he was four years old, Allan was diagnosed as having

leukemia. After several years of treatment, doctors determined that there might be hope for him if he underwent a bone marrow transplant. The family went to Seattle, Washington, for the operation. Lex was the donor for his little brother. The transplant was considered a success, and the family returned home in good spirits and resumed their lives.

"We sort of grew up with the kids ourselves, especially with Lex," said Sherry. "We always did everything together."

Several years later, Lex won a football scholarship to East Central Junior College in Mississippi. The whole family was jubilant. And when his team won a big game on the last day of September, 1983, he called his mother at three in the morning to tell her about it.

"He was so excited, and we shared that excitement," Sherry recalled. "He said he thought his team would be nationally ranked. He was on his way home for a visit before the next game."

Lex never made it home. Just a few miles outside of Calhoun, he fell asleep at the wheel and hit a truck head-on. He was killed instantly.

"On the way to the cemetery for Lex's funeral," Sherry continued, "my husband asked little Allan to look for a sign in nature that would show us that Lex was still with us. After the service at the graveside, a beautiful monarch butterfly flew between us. We believe it was a sign, and I can't think of anything more fitting than a butterfly. It is constantly on the go, just as Lex was, and it is not aggressive, and neither was our son."

When the family later redecorated their house, the wallpaper they selected was filled with butterflies.

Within a year after Lex's death, doctors discovered that Allan's leukemia has spread to his brain and spinal column.

His medication had to be discontinued to prevent further damage. The second son was dying.

"He knew he was dying, but he wasn't afraid. He knew his 'Bubba' would be waiting for him."

But Allan wasn't the only courageous member of his family. His mother and father were determined to carry on.

"We talked about the future. I even thought of seeing if I could have an operation that would allow me to have children again. But I'm too old for that," Sherry explained. "We also checked into the possibility of adopting, but there's a waiting list of several years. We have so much love to give, and we want to channel it somewhere. We know there are so many children who need it."

I asked Sherry how she and her husband had coped through their ordeal.

"We live with one thought," she said. "That God has something else planned for us. He must. He simply must."

AN OLD FOGEY WITH CLEAR VISION

My Aunt Jessie has lived in rural Georgia since 1931. She is widowed now and spends most of her time watching her "stories," which is what she calls the television soap operas. I'm not certain how old she is, and I never intend to ask, but it's a fact that she's a great-grandmother.

One of the grandchildren offered recently to take her to Atlanta to see Kenny Rogers in concert. Aunt Jessie, a lifelong devotee to country music, accepted.

Those of us who live in large urban areas learn to accept the dramatic changes which occur around us almost daily, but Aunt Jessie was shocked when she ventured from her rural security for a modern concert. It was refreshing to hear her view of it all:

"I never seen so many people in one place in my life. And when the concert finally got started, you couldn't hear a thing. Every time Kenny would start to sing, everybody would scream and holler.

"The rest of the time I couldn't see because somebody was always crawling over me to get something to eat. Looks like they would've had supper before they came to the concert, or at least brought themselves a sandwich so they wouldn't have had to leave their seats."

Aunt Jessie was amazed at the actions of some of the women at the concert. "I saw these two young girls, in britches so tight I don't know how they breathed, running all over the place, touchin' the ground just in the high places. I don't know where their mamas were. But if they had been mine, I'd have wore 'em both out for dressin' and actin' like that.

"Then there was a woman so drunk she couldn't stand up, holding a big ol' cup of beer in each hand. She could have at least stayed home if she was going to act like that.

"At the intermission I was standing in line to go to the restroom and this woman got tired of waiting, so she just pranced right into the men's room, big as you please. I thought, 'Lord, what's this world comin' to?'"

I tried to explain to Aunt Jessie that women have changed a lot since her time, and nowadays they smoke and drink in public and occasionally use profanity and generally have come a long way, baby.

"I guess I ought to be thankful for one thing," said Aunt Jessie.

"What's that?"

"That I'm still an old fogey, country woman," she said.

I'm thankful for that, too, Aunt Jessie. There aren't many of you left.

WAVING HER FLAG OF FREEDOM

We were waiting for a couple of planes. She had two, maybe three drinks. We shared a story and an opinion or two, and then she asked, "How old are you, anyway?"

"Thirty-nine," I answered.

"Same age as my husband, the sorry bastard," she said.

Ever perceptive, I asked, "You're mad at your husband?"

"Actually," she said, "he's now my ex-husband. Ran off with a girl half his age."

I made no comment. I'm old enough to know better.

"You know what's wrong with men your age?" she continued.

"Yeah," I said, "but what do you think is wrong with men my age?"

"You're all afraid of getting old, so you start chasing around after young girls." She ordered another drink. Scotch.

"How long have you been divorced?" I asked.

"Six months."

"Kids?"

"One. He's twelve. Do you know how old I am?"

When a woman asks a question like that, I always subtract five years from my best guess. "Late twenties," I answered.

"Thirty-five, and you know what's wrong with women my age?"

I had several ideas, to be sure, but the best answer at the time seemed to be shaking my head no.

"We were brought up so differently from young girls today," she began. "You take me. My mother has dominated my life. All the time I was growing up, she used to harp on me to always be a 'good girl.' And I was. I didn't dare do anything my mother wouldn't approve of. I never had a drink until I was married. I've had sex with only one man, my husband. I've been a 'good girl' all my life, and all I've got to show for it is a broken marriage and a lot of guilt."

"Yeah," I said awkwardly, "our parents sometimes leave us with a load to carry into adulthood."

"Know what I did today, though?" the woman asked. "I got dressed up in this outfit and went by my mother's house. She said, 'Oh, you look so lovely, darling. Are you going to a party?' I said, 'No, mother, I'm not going to a party. I'm going to leave here, get on an airplane and meet a man. Then I'm going to commit adultery for the first time in my life.' I thought she was going to faint. She was absolutely bewildered."

"Did she try to talk you out of it?" I wanted to know.

"I wouldn't let her. Every time she tried to preach to me, I just told her it wouldn't do any good. It's my life and I've missed so much. I've got to start being my own person, and now is as good a time as any."

She ordered one last drink. "What's so funny," she said, "is that all my mother could say to me when I left was, 'Don't do anything that will cause you to hate yourself.' If I don't do this, then I'm going to hate myself."

They called the woman's plane. She downed her drink, smiled and boarded. I hope she had a great weekend.

***

So maybe true grit has less to do with things physical and more to do with things mental. It seems to come from many sources: from religion, and sports, and living with women and dealing with living. In the words of Erskine Caldwell, "Call it experience." I've had my share.

— 5 —

Sinning and Grinning
And Knowing The
Difference

I GREW UP HEARING that good things come to those who love the Lord; the Moreland, Georgia, Methodist Church was deeply and comfortably seated in the traditional interpretation of The Word. But religion, like so many other things, isn't as simple as it used to be. Nowadays the good guys sometimes wear black and white striped hats instead of just one or the other.

Almost every day in the mail I receive a letter from some television evangelist asking me for a donation to help buy a new truck for his television equipment or to pay off the debt for the new gymnasium at New Testament University. The implication is that if I don't send them the cash, I'm on the express train for hell.

Will I end up down there with Hitler and Attila the Hun and Bonnie and Clyde just because I didn't send them five bucks for a new wrestling mat? Then again, is hell actually *down* there?

"Can you dig your way to hell?" I asked the preacher when I was a kid.

"Guess you can," he said, "but I can tell you how to get there a lot quicker."

Frankly, thinking about hell scares the you-know-where out of me. I'd much rather think about heaven. Just the other day my mail included a pamphlet entitled, "Heaven: Are You Eligible?" I took the test and scored "too close to call."

With that kind of rating, I pay close attention to all those groups who predict the coming of Judgment Day. If some guy says he has it on good authority that the end of the world is due on October 11, then I'm particularly careful that day not to do anything awful, like telling big lies, attending an adult movie or coveting my neighbor's new Porsche.

Otherwise, can you imagine your chances of getting aboard the glory train when the first question they ask you at judgment is, "For starters, what did you do today?"

"W-w-w-well, f-f-first I lied to my boss about having to go to the doctor and I went instead to see *Flesh Dance* at the Porn Palace. Then I went home and kicked the tires on my '73 Ford wagon because that's what I'm stuck with when Thorndike across the street has a new Porsche."

Take a seat, boy. The southbound leaves in just a few minutes.

I know in my heart that most of these forecasts are poppycock, but my old-fashioned upbringing always keeps me just a little uneasy. Remember, everybody thought Columbus was nuts when he bought a round-trip ticket. You just never know.

That's why I started early in life being careful not to get caught in mid-sin at the precise moment of His return. I remember my first beer. I tried to chug it down but succeeded only in gagging myself.

"What's your hurry?" asked my companion in evil.

"Beer is better when you drink it fast," I answered between coughs.

Truth is, I just wanted to finish that beer quickly so I could throw the can away and get rid of the evidence in case the Second Coming were to occur in the next five to ten minutes.

I guess it is possible to overreact to these predictions. Anytime I hear another Judgment Day date, I'm reminded of the story my grandfather used to tell about an Elmer Gantry-type preacher who came through town with his tent.

"The end is close at hand, my children," the preacher screamed one night. About that time, a small boy who had just been given a toy trumpet for his birthday walked past the tent and gave his new horn a mighty toot.

The congregation panicked and bolted out of the tent. The evangelist grabbed the cash box and cut down the street at full gallop. The little boy, wondering where everybody was headed, followed the preacher.

The preacher ran faster and faster, afraid to look back, but the little boy matched him step for step, still tooting on his new horn. Finally the preacher stopped, whipped out a switchblade and said, "Watch it, Gabe, or I'll cut you!"

My grandfather wouldn't have cared much for today's bigtime television preachers. In his oft-stated opinion, preachers were supposed to marry folks, preach funerals, mow the grass around the church and administer to the needs of the flock (that meant consoling the poor soul who lost his job, whose wife ran off, and whose trailer burned all in the same week). Our preacher even used to knock down the dirt dobbers' nests in the windows of the sanctuary so the inhabitants wouldn't bother the worshippers while he was trying to run the devil out of town on Sunday mornings.

Do you suppose that Oral Roberts or Jerry Falwell ever knocked down any dirt dobbers' nests?

My grandfather also didn't like it when younger preachers used note cards to deliver their sermons. "They ought to get it straight from the Lord," he said many a time. "Politicians use notes."

The preacher at Moreland Methodist when I was growing up suited my grandfather just fine. He drove an old car. He had only one suit. He did the yard work around the church, didn't use note cards and always attempted to answer the questions of a twelve-year-old boy when things didn't add up. Once he even preached a funeral for a dog because that little boy, who loved the dog very much, asked him to.

What would Pat Robertson say over a dog?

What bothers me today is that for every glamour boy of the pulpit, there are thousands out there who tackle the devil daily, one-on-one, with little or no audience, against long odds, and occasionally on an empty stomach.

God bless them. And God, please don't let my grandfather — I know he's around there somewhere — find out that we've got preachers down here today who use cue cards and hang out with politicians.

***

I had a dream about all this the other night. Maybe it was my grandfather passing along a little inside information. This is how it went:

God called in the angel who is in charge of keeping an eye on what's going on in the United States. "What's all this fussing about religion and politics? I thought I had Ben

Franklin and his friends work out the separation of church and state a couple of weeks ago," God said.

"Actually," said the angel, "it's been a couple of weeks heaven time, but to folks on earth it's been more than two hundred years. But every so often, they decide to argue it again."

"Who started it this time?"

"I suppose it was Jerry Falwell and the Moral Majority," answered the angel.

"Jerry who and the Moral what?"

"Jerry Falwell and the Moral Majority. Falwell is a television evangelist and he heads a fundamentalist organization called the Moral Majority. They support President Reagan because they think you are a Republican."

"Whatever gave them an idea like that?" asked God.

"They think you sent President Reagan, a Republican, to save the morals of the country because he believes in a lot of the same things as they do."

"For instance?"

"Well, President Reagan believes in prayer in public schools, and so does the Moral Majority."

"So what's the big deal? I get thousands of prayers a day from students in public schools. Here, look at this one that came in yesterday. Pretty creative for a tenth grader:"

> O Lord, hear my anxious plea.
> Algebra is killing me.
> I know not of 'x' or 'y,'
> And probably won't until the day I die.
> Please, Lord, help me at this hour
> As I take my case to the highest power.
> I care not for fame nor loot,
> Just help me find one square root.

Latin and Grammar are also trouble.
Guide me through this daily double.
And, Lord, please let me see
One passing mark in Chemistry.

Lord, why am I such a dope in school?
My teachers think I'm such a fool.
One said, 'Son, you're a horrid flop.
You bent the saw and failed at shop.'
My days in class are filled with remorse.
I can't even pass the easiest course.
I hunkered down and bowed my neck,
But I burnt the cake and flagged Home Ec.

In English Lit, I studied hard
And read all the words of the Bard.
But my mind is like a hateful Judas.
It couldn't recall, 'Et tu, Brutus?'

Lord, will there ever be
A tougher subject than History?
Into the past I steadfastly delve,
From Plymouth Rock to 1812.
I learn of all those patriotic folk,
From John Q. Adams to James K. Polk.
But test time comes and I fall on my tail.
Was it Patrick Henry or Nathan Hale?

Lord, must I offer an apology
For three times failing Biology?
Why is it I'm in such a fog
Concerning the innards of a frog?
I push and strive and strain and grope

To come to terms with the microscope.
Lord, please forgive my derision,
But who gives a hoot for cellular division?

Lord, I wish that I could vanish
When the teacher calls on me in Spanish.
And I promise, it's a cinch,
I'll never learn a word of French.

Down in gym I take P.E.
Calisthenics will be the death of me.
I have all the grace of a mop.
I made an 'F' in side straddle hop.

Lord, is there anything I can't flub?
Will I ever be in Beta Club?
I have never found the key to knowledge,
And my folks want me to go to college.
Oh, such a thing I constantly dread.
I'd as soon join the Marines instead.
Lord, please give me a sign
That you've been listening all this time.
If you will help, I'll give my all,
And won't even chew gum in study hall.
Please lead me out of this constant coma,
And give me a chance at my diploma.
Let others fight about church and state.
I pray only to graduate. Amen.

"Now, that's a prayer worthy of my time," said God. "But apparently that's not good enough for this Falwell fellow. Tell me more about him."

"Well, he has his own television show."

"When does he visit the sick?"

"He doesn't have time for that. If he's not preaching on the air, he's busy fund raising for his ministry or else he's on one of those news shows like, 'This Week With David Brinkley,' telling people where you stand on this and that."

"Just what I needed," said God, "another spokesman." God thought for a moment and then said to the angel, "I want you to do something for me. I want you to deliver a few messages. First, tell both sides that I don't want to be any part of their political squabble. Their forefathers had the good sense to leave me out of politics, and I don't see why they can't.

"Also, tell Reagan to forget about school prayer for awhile and instead find a way to talk to the Russians before they find a way to destroy what I've created. Then tell that Falwell fellow to stop using my name to boost his television ratings and stop trying to run the country from his pulpit. Can you handle all that?" God asked the angel.

"Yes, ma'am," the angel replied.

***

Apparently that message I dreamed hasn't been delivered quite yet, because the Moral Majority is still busy trying to convince us that they have all the answers. Me, I'm more confused than ever. It's gotten to the point that I'm not sure I know sin when I see it. Or hear it. According to the Moral Majority, music is one of the major mediums of the devil today, and nowhere is the temperature hotter than in country music.

I'll be the first to admit that some questionable lyrics have sneaked into country music in recent years, but are the dials "down there" really tuned to WSM? In an attempt to get this disturbing issue cleared up, I contacted Mrs. Debbie Sue Ann Betty Jo Jenkins of Blue Ball, Arkansas. She's the

Moral Majority's expert on the state of country music.

"May I call you Debbie Sue Ann Betty Jo?" I asked when I reached her on the phone.

"Call me anything but 'Barracuda,'" she replied. "That's what Conway Twitty called me when I tried to stop his show in Little Rock."

"You tried to stop the Conway Twitty show?"

"He was singing that trashy song about meeting a woman in a bar who was wearing tight britches," Mrs. Jenkins explained.

I know the song in question, entitled "Tight-fittin' Jeans," and I suppose it is a little suggestive. I asked Mrs. Jenkins which part of the song offended her most.

"The part where the woman tells Conway Twitty, 'Pardner, there's a tiger in these tight-fittin' jeans.'"

I quickly realized that Debbie Sue Ann Betty Jo, Mrs. Jenkins, was a bit of a tiger herself. Anybody who would try to stop Conway Twitty as he groaned to his legion of fans is not the sort of person to be taken lightly.

"What other songs offend the Moral Majority?" I asked.

"Anything by Barbara Mandrell," she said.

Barbara Mandrell a musical filth peddler? I couldn't believe it.

"Imagine such perversion as inviting a man to eat crackers in bed with you in a song," explained Mrs. Jenkins, referring of course to Ms. Mandrell's hit song, "You Can Eat Crackers in My Bed Anytime." She continued, "Decent people would never do such a thing. Beds are for sleeping and nothing else."

"What does Mr. Jenkins think about that?" I asked.

"He doesn't even like crackers," she said.

Mrs. Jenkins went on to list several other songs which the Moral Majority disapproves of:

- "My Favorite Memory" by Merle Haggard. One line recalls "sleeping all night long on the floor." "Probably ate a bunch of crackers before they dozed off," said Mrs. Jenkins.
- "Best Bedroom in Town" by Tammy Wynette. "Doesn't anybody ever get out of bed in Nashville?" asked Mrs. Jenkins.
- "If I Said You Had a Beautiful Body Would You Hold It Against Me?" by the Bellamy Brothers. "Utter trash," said Mrs. Jenkins. "I'll bet their mother, Mrs. Bellamy, hides herself in shame every time she hears that song. If Mr. Jenkins had ever said anything like that to me, I would have bashed in his little worm head."
- "My Baby Thinks He's a Train" by Rosanne Cash. "More perversion," explained Mrs. Jenkins. "Mr. Jenkins decided he was a Greyhound bus once and that he was leaving."

"What did you do?" I asked her.

"Bashed in his little worm head, of course."

Finally I asked Mrs. Jenkins to name the one song which she feels is most harmful.

"It's by Glen Campbell," she said.

"Glen Campbell?"

"Yes, I know it's hard to believe, but he sings a song called, 'I Love My Truck.' Can you imagine a nice boy from Arkansas getting involved in something like that?"

No, ma'am, I sure can't.

***

Gospel music, thank the Lord and Mrs. Jenkins, is still safe from such perversion, and I listen to it with gusto and a clean conscience. I get my interest in gospel music honestly. My late father could hunker down on a piano and make it sing a joyful noise as long as there was somebody around to listen.

My Uncle Dorsey on my mother's side rarely missed an all-night gospel sing at the old Atlanta Municipal Auditorium. He favored the bass singer, the tall fellow in the back who always let go on the "Wellawella's," as in, "Wellawella, evuhbody's gon' have a livin' in glowry...."

I grew up in my maternal grandmother's house, and each Sunday morning I awakened to her radio blaring out the "Gospel Jubilee." My grandmother preferred the inevitable short, baby-faced tenor in the quartet who could pop up there higher than a kite with a nearly operatic, "He's my Jeeeeesus!"

Recently I attended the National Gospel Quartet Convention in Nashville, Tennessee, and it was a glooorious event. The auditorium was encircled by those rolling motels that once were Greyhound buses, carrying groups from date to date. On the sides were the names of the groups — the Singing Echoes, the Kingsmen, this family and that.

The auditorium was maybe half full when I entered, but before the night was over it was bulging. In the hallways were booths where gospel fans could buy tapes and albums and autographed photos of their favorite performers. As each quartet left the stage, a spokesperson was given the opportunity to plug the group's wares:

"We're right over yonder at booth fifteen," a man shouted into the microphone, "and we got a three-album-for-fifteen-dollar sale on. Y'all drop by to see us."

There was passion in the music. It jumped and even rocked a bit, and it set toes to tapping and occasionally brought the audience to its feet, heads held toward the heavens, hands clapping.

"We ain't the stars of the show," a fellow said. "Jesus is the star. Let's all stand and give Him a hand!"

Another group walked on, and the lead singer said, "I

61

seen on the marquee out front that the Talking Heads are coming to this auditorium. There's gonna be dope-smokin', pill-poppin' and rock music. But you ain't gonna get none of that here tonight. All you gonna get high on is Jeeeesus!"

The crowd loved it.

The last group appeared on the stage and sang its hit song, "Call Me What You Want To, But When He Calls Me, Call Me Gone." The crowd roared following a rousing rendition.

"Sort of gives you glowry bumps listenin' to 'em, don't it?" said the woman sitting next to me.

It does at that. It sure does.

— 6 —

Are You Non-Essential, Undesirable, Unmentionable Or Just Undone?

SOMETIMES YOU DON'T have to go out of your way to find opportunities to develop true grit. They'll come to you. Just surviving the lunacy and frustrations of the modern world is evidence of some degree of character. Isn't that why our society always makes such a big deal out of golden wedding anniversaries?

In my particular situation, I travel a lot. Thirty years ago that would have meant many pleasurable train rides with good food, good drink and plenty of time to read or relax. Today, however, it means airports and airplanes and endless delays and migraine headaches. It starts before you even leave home.

"Good morning. Wingandaprayer Airlines. May I help you?"

"Yes," I said to the voice on the phone. "I'd like to make two round-trip reservations for the Sunday evening flight to

Pittsburgh, please."

"Will this be first class, tourist or Wingandaprayer's new cargo class?" she asked.

"Cargo class?"

"Certainly, sir. In an effort to attract your business in these competitive times, Wingandaprayer Airlines is offering an innovative and inexpensive way for you to travel by air. Cargo class simply means you ride in the cargo hold with the baggage at a huge savings in cost. This is available, however, only to those passengers who will fit into their own hanging bags."

"I'll just take tourist," I said.

"Oxygen or non-oxygen?"

"I don't understand."

"Another Wingandaprayer option in our effort to offer passengers a variety of ways to save money and still not have to take the bus," she explained. "If you prefer to bring your own oxygen tank, then your seat will not be equipped with an automatic oxygen mask release in case of sudden cabin depressurization. If Wingandaprayer doesn't have to provide you with oxygen, it can save money and pass those savings along to its customers in the form of reduced fares."

"But I don't have my own oxygen tank."

"In that case, sir, how long can you hold your breath?"

"I'll just take two seats with oxygen."

"Will you be traveling with your wife or another adult?"

"No, I'll be traveling with my nephew Robert, who's six."

"Does he chew Rootie-Tootie Bubble Gum?"

"Is that the kind that turns his teeth blue?" I asked.

"Exactly, sir, and Wingandaprayer now offers free tickets to children if they show eight Rootie-Tootie Bubble Gum wrappers when they go to the agent for their boarding passes. 'Get 'em while they're young and they're yours forever,' is what we always say at Wingandaprayer," she explained.

"So what is the adult fare?"

"Depends, sir. Will you be cashing in coupons on this trip?"

"Coupons?"

"Check your local newspaper for Wingandaprayer cost-cutting coupons. Bring the coupons with you to the ticket agent and trade them in for savings on your fare."

"OK. Now, will dinner be served on the evening flight to Pittsburgh?"

"Not in tourist, sir. Wingandaprayer lost millions last year, and in an effort to keep our own costs down, we've cut out all meal service except in first class, where passengers are allowed to bob for apples."

"I'll pack a sandwich for me and Robert. Now, will you please see if there is space available on the evening flight to Pittsburgh?"

"I have you confirmed on our 7:20 flight to Pittsburgh, sir. May I have your home address?"

"Why do you need my home address?" I asked.

"So Wingandaprayer can mail you your green stamps and toaster."

When we finally arrived at the airport and boarded the plane, we were immediately greeted by two delays. The first, said the captain, was due to "a minor mechanical problem. We should have it cleared up soon." If an airplane is going to develop a mechanical problem, whether major or minor, the best time to do so is when it's still on the ground. Nonetheless, it can be extremely unsettling to the passengers.

For example, what does the captain consider "minor"? It could be anything from a wing being loose to the navigator's pen being out of ink. Secondly, how can the captain or the passengers know for sure that the problem has been fixed? It's not exactly like dealing with someone's pickup truck, where the mechanic opens the hood, pulls at a few wires and hoses, and then says, "Try it now." If the truck doesn't start, the mechanic pulls at some different wires and hoses. With an airplane, you don't get a second chance.

I expressed my concern to a passing stewardess.

"Don't worry," she said, "our mechanic knows this plane from front to back."

If he knows so much, I thought to myself, why isn't he in the cockpit flying this sucker instead of underneath it pulling at wires and hoses? I looked out the window and saw a fellow who looked like a mechanic scratching his head with a big wrench. On his breast pocket I could read the name, Bobby Earl. Would you trust your life to a man named Bobby Earl?

Another concern was that we were flying on Sunday. Have you ever tried to find a mechanic to work on your car on Sunday? The only ones I've ever found had just been fired from Brake-O. Bobby Earl worked on the plane for about an hour. Then I heard him yell to the pilot, "Try it now!" Sure enough, it started. I didn't know whether to be happy or sad.

As we backed away from the terminal (Why do they have to call it that?), the chief stewardess announced another delay.

"Due to heavy traffic here at the airport, we are presently 108th in line for takeoff, which means we're going to spend approximately the four hours and ten minutes either taxiing slowly or sitting in line with a bunch of other planes waiting to take off," she explained.

"Wingandaprayer Airlines would like to apologize for

this inconvenience. We realize that some of you have connections or important meetings in Pittsburgh and that this sort of delay could cause you to lose your company's biggest account, among other disastrous occurrences. But please do not whine, because we can't help it if thirty-five other airlines decided to schedule takeoffs at the same time we did.

"We will do everything in our power to make up for this excruciating experience. For those of you who might want to read while we are taxiing out, ask your flight attendant to bring you something from Wingandaprayer's in-flight library. Available today are *War and Peace*, *The Rise and Fall of the Third Reich*, and *The Complete Works of Victor Hugo*.

"Later in our taxi out, we will be offering at no charge our 'Movie While You Wait.' Our feature in first class will be the original, uncut version of *Gone With the Wind*, while our coach passengers will enjoy viewing *Rocky I, II* and *III*.

"If we still haven't taken off by that time, Wingandaprayer has other means of killing time for our passengers. There will be a bridge tournament in rows twenty-five through thirty. For those who prefer bingo, cards may be purchased at a nominal charge. First officer Willard Smith, who is just as bored as the rest of you, will be calling the games in rows seven through twenty-four.

"In first class there will be Trivial Pursuit games and mud wrestling for any passengers who are interested, as well as a musical performance by two of our flight attendants, Ramona Dentz and Glenda Jane Chastain, singing songs they actually wrote, such as, 'I've Got the Air Sickness Bag Blues.' Other pre-takeoff performances include a lecture by Captain Allis Chalmers, who will explain how to hot-wire a 747, and a demonstration on in-flight macramé by navigator Marco Polonski.

"Also, because of our long delay, our smoking passengers may wish to step outside to smoke. If so, please remember to walk along with the aircraft in case it moves so you don't get too far behind. Thank you for ridin — , I mean flying, Wingandaprayer Airlines, and have a pleasant flight."

***

If dealing with airlines doesn't test your mettle and cultivate a little true grit, then try buying or selling a house. Real estate agents are God's curse on mankind when locusts are out of season.

When you're trying to buy a house, there are basically three parties involved: (1) a large lending agency which employs no people, only computers, (2) a real estate agent, who is one of seventeen zillion housewives who got bored with Tuesday morning doubles and went out and got licensed to sell houses, and (3) a working stiff with a wife and two kids.

Here's how the game is played:

The stiff and his wife and two kids have outgrown their modest, 2BR, 1BA, brk. rch. w/o fpl. They are looking for something a little nicer and with more space. They contact a real estate agent, an attractive person named Delores who smokes a lot and drives a late-model Mercedes.

Delores takes the stiff and his wife and his two kids to look at houses that are for sale. The stiff is shown a house with three bedrooms, two baths and a fireplace in the den, which is exactly what he had in mind. Last year it cost $17,000. But that was last year.

"This honey of a place is one-five," says Delores. "One-five" is real estate saleslady talk for one hundred and five big ones. I'm talking thousands.

The poor stiff, meanwhile, is holding about half of the downpayment and facing an interest rate that would make

Shylock cringe.

"But, Darling," says his wife, "it's just perfect, and Marvin and Arnold (the two kids) can each have their own bedroom."

"Yeah, Dad," echo Marvin and Arnold.

This is where the real estate game gets interesting. There's no way the stiff can do what his father probably did — plunk down ten percent and make reasonable payments the rest of his life — so he has to engage in what is termed "creative financing." That's real estate saleslady talk for, "No way you can afford this house, turkey, but I haven't had a good commission in a month, so here's the way we're going to rig it."

There are all sorts of ways to finance a house creatively. Here are a few:

• LOAN ASSUMPTION — That's where you assume your brother-in-law, the doctor, will lend you the money for a downpayment, but he laughs in your face and asks if Marvin and Arnold can come over to help him clean his pool.

• WRAPAROUND MORTGAGE — That's where a bunch of fast-talking guys with cigars wrap you around their little fingers and you're in so deep you have to take a night job and Marvin and Arnold forget you exist.

• GRADUATED PAYMENTS — The first year you pay ten dollars a month. The next year you pay ten thousand dollars a month. The following year you live in a tent.

• STARVATION MORTGAGE PLAN — You can make your house payments, but you can't afford food for the first two years of the loan. Marvin and Arnold go to live with your brother-in-law.

• BLACKMAIL — You find out the owner of the house you are trying to buy had a sex-change operation in 1963.

"He" gives you the house for free and buys Marvin and Arnold a dog.

• ROB-A-LIQUOR-STORE PLAN — Just what the name implies. You rob liquor stores until you can afford the house. The real estate firm locates the stores and furnishes a stocking to go over your head. Marvin and Arnold watch the doors. Delores drives the getaway car.

Selling a house can be equally frustrating. First the house sits for six months without a single person coming to look at it, but Delores is still nauseatingly optimistic.

This house will sell. I guarantee it," she says, jingling the change in her pocket and rocking back and forth on her heels.

"Yeah, but during my lifetime?" asks the stiff.

"Trust me," says Delores, popping her gum. Didn't I buy a Pinto from her several years ago? Or was she the travel agent who sold me the Braniff charter to West Beirut?

Finally one afternoon the phone rings and Delores says, "Will it be OK to show the house later today?" What that really means is, "I'll be there in four minutes. These turkeys (prospective buyers) could be hot."

Delores's timing is magnificent. The United States Army Mule Team and its drivers were over for lunch and have just left, and she wants to show the house in four minutes.

"It'll just take me a week to hose the place down," you argue.

"Trust me," says Delores. The Pinto was lemon yellow and the engine sounded like it had emphysema.

The stiff immediately starts throwing things under chairs, under the sofa, into cabinets, and his wife puts something on the stove to boil. That's another tip from Delores: boil cinnamon to give the house a "homey" smell.

"What's that god-awful smell?" asks the man as soon as

he walks through the front door.

"Smells like cinnamon to me," says his wife.

"I can't stand the smell of cinnamon. Let's go back and take another look at that house that smelled like garlic. You know, I just love garlic."

Another trick Delores suggests is to have a fire burning in the fireplace. Gives the house a "cozy" feeling, she says.

Only problem is that stiff forgets to open the flue.

"Stay close to the floor and there's plenty of air," says Delores to the prospective buyers. "Now, in there is the master bedroom...."

"Let's get out of here," the man says to his wife. "I'll call the fire department at the first pay phone we see."

I once had a house that sat for nine months without selling. Without so much as thinking about selling. So I did what any self-respecting syndicated columnist would do: I wrote a column about an eccentric old bird who lived there before me and buried $200,000 in cash somewhere on the property just before he died. With my bad back, I couldn't even lift a shovel, I wrote, but . . .

In the words of Delores, "Trust me."

***

Unfortunately, those sorts of shenanigans are not limited to the real estate industry. Deception and misrepresentation are more prevalent today than Boy George. Our very language is twisted and distorted daily so that it's hard to know exactly what phrases mean anymore. Take politics, for example.

When a politician says, "We're still checking the results of our latest poll," what he really means is, "I paid a fortuneteller fifty bucks to predict my chances, and she said that if I got two thousand votes she'd eat her crystal ball."

Here are some of their other favorites:

- "A heavy turnout will help us." If all my cousins bother to vote, I might hit double figures.
- "I think bad weather on election day would definitely benefit my opponent." My support is so weak that I'll lose half my votes if there's more than a ten percent chance of rain.
- "We haven't had any attention from the media." I bought drinks for two television reporters and a newspaper columnist, and all I got in return was stuck with a fifty-dollar tab.
- "I don't know how my opponent could stoop so low as to bring up something like that." You rig just one little million-dollar construction bid and everybody wants to make a federal case out of it.
- "We've run a clean, honest campaign." I spent $25,000 on private detective fees and couldn't come up with a damn thing on my opponent.
- "No matter what the outcome of the election, we've made a lot of new friends all over the country." Especially the blonde at the bar at the Hyatt in San Francisco.
- "I have nothing to be ashamed of." I gave the blonde a ficticious name.
- "You can't run a campaign as inexpensively as you once could." Votes aren't nearly as cheap as they used to be.
- "I'm just a simple country boy." The closest I ever got to a cow was ordering Steak Diane at the country club.
- "It's too early to make any sort of definitive statement on how the election is going." My campaign manager hasn't returned with the booze yet.
- "I want to thank my wife for all her support during the campaign." She believed the story about the lipstick on my shirt after the campaign trip to San Francisco.
- "I would like to congratulate my opponent on his vic-

tory." All I want is five minutes alone with that sorry SOB.

- "Now that the campaign is over, I'm looking forward to getting my life back to normal." I'm not going to sober up for a week.
- "The people have spoken." If I'd known I had that many enemies, I'd have carried a gun.

Politicians and their aides also are forever coming up with catch words or phrases which I find terribly confusing. For example, not long ago President Reagan sent home a lot of "non-essential" government employees because he was fighting with Congress about getting a budget approved.

After his announcement, I couldn't help wondering, What do all those non-essential government employees do? I suppose they handle all the non-essential work the government has to do. But if thousands of government employees are non-essential, what about me? How do I know if I'm essential to the country or not?

To help myself and other Americans answer this crucial question, I devised a test to find out if you're non-essential or not. Just answer the following questions.

1. Is it absolutely necessary that you stay awake and in an upright position while performing your duties?

2. If you walked into the boss's office and demanded a raise, would he (a) give you the raise? (b) throw you out of his office? (c) mistake you for Killingsworth from accounting who died last year?

3. If you took a leave of absence and hiked the Appalachian Trail for six months and came back to work with a full beard, would anybody notice that you had been away, or, if you're female, remark how it's not everyday that you see a woman with a full beard?

4. Are you with the Ford Motor Company and presently designing a diesel Edsel?

5. If you called in sick, would the boss hire a temporary to fill in, or would he say, "Killingsworth from accounting can handle things until you get back"?

6. If you said, "But, sir, Killingsworth from accounting died last year," would the boss respond, "Too bad, he was a good man," or, "I know. That's why he'd be perfect for your job"?

7. Are you Woody Allen's weight coach?

8. If one day you didn't come to work but sent your dog instead, what most likely would happen? (a) Nobody would notice the difference; (b) The SPCA would cite you for unnecessarily boring a defenseless animal; (c) Your dog would be promoted because he was overqualified for your job.

Finally, if you had the time to take this test while at work, it's a good bet you're non-essential.

Another category of people frequently referred to by the Reagan Administration is "undesirables." You might recall several years ago when a former Secretary of the Interior suggested that The Beach Boys might attract "undesirables" to a Washington concert. The Beach Boys, incidentally, are still going strong; the former Secretary now is a fur trapper on the upper east side of Manhattan.

About that same time officials at the University of Texas opposed a Willie Nelson concert on campus because he might attract "undesirables." Since I am one of Willie's biggest fans and attend his concerts at every opportunity, does that make me an undesirable?

Once again, I devised a test to help me and other confused Americans to discover if we are, in fact, undesirable.

Just answer truthfully the following questions.

1. When you hear Willie Nelson sing "Up Against the Wall, You Redneck Mother," does it make you want to (a) beat up a hippie; (b) drink beer from a quart jar; (c) take off your shirt; (d) call your mom?

2. Does The Beach Boys's "Little Surfer Girl" make you want to (a) take narcotics; (b) quit your job and go live at the beach; (c) insult a policeman; (d) ice down some Pepsi and build a sand castle?

3. If you were to attend a Beach Boys concert, which of the following would you likely wear? (a) half a bikini; (b) T-shirt with an obscene message; (c) it doesn't matter because you're going to take it off as soon as you get good and drunk anyway; (d) Gray Flannel cologne.

4. The last time you saw a Willie Nelson concert, which of the following best describes your behavior? (a) loud and obnoxious; (b) nasty and mean; (c) it took a dozen cops to get you into the paddy wagon; (d) you read the latest issue of the *New Yorker* between numbers.

5. Which of the following do you think would come in most handy at your next Beach Boys concert? (a) a hand grenade; (b) your coke dealer; (c) assorted birth control devices; (d) an uncrowded restroom.

6. Which of the the following would you be most likely to do after attending a Willie Nelson concert? (a) get tattooed; (b) burn a city; (c) rape and pillage; (d) watch "Nightline."

That's it; you can relax now. If you answered (d) to all of the questions, you most certainly are not an undesirable. If you did not answer any questions with (d), you're invited to a party at my house next Saturday night. Dress is not required.

***

It seems to me that a lot of old-fashioned jobs have been declared non-essential or else those who worked them have been deemed undesirable. For example, what has happened to movie ushers?

It used to be that you bought your ticket and some popcorn and a nice young man in a uniform would lead you with his flashlight to an available seat. You think that wasn't an essential job? You walk into a dark movie theater these days and there's no telling what can happen. You might sit next to a weirdo who makes sucking noises with his teeth. Or worse, you could sit on top of somebody. I walked into a dark theater the other day and was about to comment on how soft and comfortable the seats were when I realized I was sitting on a fat woman's lap.

"Get off me, you weirdo!" she screamed. I scrambled away and landed in another seat on top of a small child, who pinched me. I finally found an empty seat and made sucking noises with my teeth so that I'd be left alone.

And whatever happened to the old-timey car washes? Who declared them non-essential? Years ago people at a carwash would attack your auto with brushes and rags, and then they'd sweep and vacuum the inside of the car. Not even the Methodist Youth Fellowship car washes do that anymore. It's important to have the inside of your car cleaned occasionally. I did so recently and found two dollars in change, a missing tennis shoe and an old friend I thought had moved to Wyoming.

In today's automatic car washes, I feel like I'm trapped inside a giant washing machine like a pair of soiled pajamas about to be rinsed to death. If the inside gets cleaned, it's only because my windows leak and the jet sprays soak the interior.

And where, pray tell, are the old door-to-door salesmen?

Nobody comes to my house selling magazines or encyclopedias or vacuum cleaners anymore.

"Hi," the young man would say. "My name is Harvey and I'm working my way through college and I'm trying to win this contest...."

I don't remember ever buying anything from those salesmen, but at least it kept them off the streets and gave the dogs a little sport that was safer than chasing cars. What could be more essential?

In place of those important old jobs, we now have people doing the most absurd jobs imaginable. Just who are those people in the bathrooms everywhere I go? Do their wives know what they're doing?

I've been able to go to the bathroom without assistance since I was five or six, but lately every time I turn around I'm confronted by a smiling, grown man bearing towels. For the use of one, I'm expected to drop something spendable into his tip dish. I admit that I'm not very mechanically inclined, but I can usually figure out a towel dispenser or even one of those electric blowers without help.

There are, of course, ways to avoid restroom attendants. You can leave quickly without washing your hands, or you can simply hand the towel back to the attendant, smile and say thank you. If he still wants a tip, tell him to plant his corn early next year.

Not washing your hands can be unsanitary, however, or even unsociable. I was standing at a urinal beside two fellows at a Georgia-Auburn football game once. The Georgia fan, dressed in red and black from head to toe, finished his business, zipped his pants and headed for the door.

"Hey, Bulldog," shouted the Auburn fan, "don't they teach you guys at Georgia to wash after using the bathroom?"

"No," said the Bulldog fan, "they teach us not to piss on our hands."

I'm a dyed-in-the-wool Bulldog, and that's why I don't need anybody in the bathroom handing me a towel.

***

Being non-essential, undesirable or even outmoded is minor compared to the shame that can result from being associated with unmentionables. I'm not referring to disreputable characters, but rather to women's lingerie. Buying it, even for your wife, can be more embarrassing than urinals that splash.

In the first place, you never know who might see you.

"Guess who I saw in Willoughby's buying lingerie," says one busybody to another.

"Who?"

"Harvey Nelson, that's who."

"Never would have figured him for the kinky type."

"I feel sorry for his poor wife and children."

You can't walk into a lingerie department with a big grin on your face and say, "I'm not buying these for myself," because everyone will assume that you certainly are; neither can you walk in announcing, "These are for my wife, you know," because everyone will assume that they certainly are not. In such situations, I recommend a disguise, such as wearing dark glasses and speaking with a foreign accent.

"May I help you, sir?" the saleslady will ask.

"*Si*," you answer. "I would like to look at your nightgown collection, *por favor.*"

The saleslady will have no idea she is selling good ol' Harvey Nelson something that the Catwoman on Bourbon Street wouldn't wear.

"I'll tell you something, Mildred," she'll say to her friend at lunch. "Those French are everything they say they are."

There are a couple more "don'ts" which I would recommend to any man who finds himself in this situation:

• Don't ask the saleslady to try on lingerie "since you're about the same size as my wife."

• Don't inquire about the possibility of purchasing the especially attractive mannequin in the black nightie. This could lead to an embarrassing arrest.

• Don't buy your wife or mistress colored underpants with the days of the week or the Clemson football schedule printed on them. For some reason, most women don't like them.

***

One of the greatest personal adversities I must endure, one that develops patience and grit in me, is the frequent abuse of my last name. A man's name is his birthright, and to have it besmudged is a terrible thing.

Only recently someone sent me an advertisement from the local newspaper in which a grocery store was offering "Fresh Chicken Grizzards" at seventy-nine cents a pound. The loving folks who sent me the ad included a notation: "Know the difference between a gizzard and a grizzard? One's just part of a chicken. The other is the whole thing."

To think that riffraff like that are allowed to use the public mails.

What obviously happened in the ad was that someone made a small error. By inserting an *r* in gizzards (which aren't worth seventy-nine cents a pound, no matter how you spell 'em), they libeled my proud name. It's not the first time, I must admit. People of little breeding often pronounce my name without the *r*. In restaurants they're always blurting out, "Gizzard, party of four. The Gizzard party, please." I save a lot of money on tips when that

79

happens.

Other people simply mispronounce the name by making it rhyme with lizard. It does not. Notice the two z's, which means that Grizzard should be pronounced GrizZARD, which is French in origin and means "wild stallion."

There have been some very famous GrizZARDS down through the years who have made the name synonymous with noble deeds and glory. There was Pierre GrizZARD, a famous French sheetrocker who is given credit for many of the aesthetic qualities of the Palace of Versailles.

Then there was Jean Paul GrizZARD, the French trapper who single-handedly introduced several different strains of venereal disease to the North American Indians in the middle of the eighteenth century.

And, of course, there was my great, great, great grand-father, Brigadier General Beauregard GrizZARD of the Confederate Army, who successfully defended Miami Beach against the yankees during the Civil War, something no one else has been able to do since.

Yes, mine is a proud name, steeped in history and tradition. To have it abused in some grocery ad is a personal affront to me and my kin. And for anyone who is thinking about writing me a letter referring to that insidious joke about Mr. BuzZARD who's in the yard, and Mr. TurTELL who's at the well, and Mr. RabBIT, etc., don't bother. Mr. GrizZARD has already heard it a million times.

***

Of all the trials and tribulations I face, one of the most difficult certainly is Sunday nights. I hate Sunday nights. I think this hatred goes back to my childhood.

Sunday mornings when I was growing up were wonderful. We got up early with the radio blaring gospel music through the house, ate a wonderful breakfast of homemade biscuits and ham or bacon and then got ready for Sunday school.

I had only one white shirt and wore it every Sunday. My mother would wash it, hang it on the line to dry in the Southern sunshine and then iron it by hand. There is a special place in heaven for women who spent days of their lives ironing.

Sunday school itself was a social event. They put us kids in the basement and for an hour we sang songs like, "Do, Lord, oh do, Lord, oh do remember me, praise Jesus!" The sermon hour wasn't as easy. I watched the hands on my mother's watch crawl as I drew hills and birds on the title pages of the hymnals. I hope the Great Scorer doesn't hold that against me; I was only nine.

Then came that wonderful Sunday lunch, featuring fried chicken and rice and gravy and plump prizes from the garden. And, of course, more homemade biscuits. My mother always let me fork the first piece of white meat. I hope someday I love a child enough to let them do the same.

On Sunday afternoons my friends and I dammed creeks and watched trains or rode bikes or hit rocks with broom handles. Then as the sun got low in the sky, we'd gather on the front porch and start talking about supper. But it was never an organized meal — just leftover chicken and biscuits whenever you wanted it.

I think that's where my problem with Sunday evenings began. I was a grown man before I stopped pouting that my mother made me get my own supper on Sunday evenings. Inevitably there was no white meat left, only dark. And the only thing on television was Ed Sullivan with seals and jugglers. It was a depressing way to end what had been a wonderful day.

Sunday nights still feel the same way. They depress me. I take a lot of Sunday night meals alone these days, and many times I would be thankful for a cold piece of dark meat. There's still nothing much on TV, just an occasional "60 Minutes" piece on germ warfare that depresses me even more.

There's a distinct quiet on Sunday nights. A lonely quiet. I get sentimental. I call a few old friends, we talk, hang up and the quiet is even quieter. I try to work a lick but my mind won't have it. It's too late to call anyone else. I eat some tuna fish straight from the can.

I also pray on Sunday nights, whether I feel the need to or not. Give Monday a little shove, Lord. Do.

***

Finally, for those citizens of the world who endure it daily, who confront idiocy and walk away from it a better man or woman for having done so, I offer some questions and answers that don't necessarily match but are worthy of your consideration nonetheless.

THE QUESTIONS:
- Why is it that no matter which lane you're in on the expressway, the other one is always moving faster?
- Who ate the first oyster?
- Who said convenience stores are convenient? As compared to what?
- Why do service stations lock the bathroom door but leave the cash register unlocked?
- Is it really necessary for bowling balls to be that heavy?
- Do animals go to heaven when they die?
- Did Michael Jackson or Boy George every play any sports?
- What are chicken fingers that so many restaurants are

serving these days? I didn't know they had fingers.

• Why is it I have sixty channels on my television and still can't find anything worth watching?

• What makes popcorn pop?

• What happened to the power in modern automobiles? They're wonderful for funeral processions but no match for a strong headwind.

• Why aren't there any black hockey players?

• What are those little green things in fruitcake?

THE ANSWERS:

• Most of the things your mother told you are true. Disregard the part about eating liver to live longer; it's not worth it.

• Life isn't fair. That's what makes it so interesting.

• Money doesn't grow on trees, and if it did somebody else would own the orchard.

• If you have to shoot it, don't drink it.

• The greatest benefit of going to college is learning to get up in the morning without somebody making you.

• Going to church on Sunday morning will make you feel better no matter what you did on Saturday night.

• The best things in life aren't free. Just ask any poor person.

• Never buy anything from a man who jingles his change.

• If you can't flow, flee.

— 7 —

One Man's Hominy Is Another Man's Grit

Another War, Another Legacy

HE CAME WALKING ACROSS the lobby of the hotel. He was scraggly and his jeans were in need of a washing. He carried a paper sack.

He hit on the cashier first. She shooed him away with a flick of her wrist. A woman sat reading in a chair. He approached her. She looked up from her magazine only for a second and then went back to reading, ignoring his pitch. Then he saw me. If you panhandle long enough, I suppose it becomes easy to spot a soft touch.

"Sir," he began, "I wonder if I could speak with you for a moment?"

Most beggars are very polite. They can't afford not to be. He started to reach inside his sack.

"What are you selling?" I asked.

"I'm not selling anything. I'm just asking for a donation for this."

85

He handed me a lapel pin, a tiny American flag. The pin was attached to a card which read, "Show your colors and help a disabled veteran."

"You're a disabled veteran?" I asked the man.

"Got my card to prove it."

He pulled a tattered wallet out of his back pocket and drew out a small card. On the card, he or someone else had scrawled, "Charles Ienberg, Disabled Vet."

"World War II?" I continued.

"I ain't that old," he said. "Korea."

His breath smelled like stale beer. I thought of another man I knew who also fought in Korea and drank after he came back.

"Were you wounded?" I went on.

"See this fingernail?" he said, pointing the index finger on his right hand toward me. "They pulled the fingernail off and burned my hands with cigarettes."

"Who is 'they?'"

"North Koreans," he answered. "I jumped into South Korea and they got me and these three other fellows just like that. When we finally got out, they sent me to Seattle and I was in the hospital for a long time. I never have been the same since. They told me to quit drinking, but that ain't no easy thing to do."

"You're still drinking?"

"I'll be honest with you, sir," he said, "I need me a drink pretty bad right now. I ain't gonna lie to you. I'm hungry, but I need a drink a lot worse than I need something to eat."

I appreciated his honesty. "This is all you do, ask for donations for these pins?" I asked.

"Used to do some house painting, but I can't get no work no more. Guess I'm too old."

"How old are you?"

"Fifty-two."

He looked twenty years older than that. I pulled a five out of my pocket and handed it to him. He handed me a lapel pin. Then he thanked me for my donation, tucked his sack back under his arm and shuffled away to buy his pint.

I mentioned another lonely old soldier. I used to give him whiskey money, too. I buried him next to his mother.

Damn wars. Damn them all.

LIVING UP TO HIS CREED

When Chuck joined the Boy Scouts at age fourteen, the kids at school gave him a lot of grief about it. It wasn't exactly a groovy thing to do, joining the Scouts, especially at that mature age. "It was pretty rough on him," Chuck's scoutmaster told me.

I've forgotten all of the Boy Scout creed, but I remember that "kind" was in there somewhere. Chuck's scoutmaster recalled the time his troop was on a camping trip and Chuck found a dead mother squirrel with a lot of hungry babies in the nest. He took the babies home and fed them with an eyedropper until they were strong enough to tackle the forest on their own. That sort of thing gets out at school and a fellow might never live it down.

Chuck joined a scouting group called the Leadership Corps, where older kids teach intermediate Scouts special skills. Chuck's special skills were canoeing and swimming. So not long ago Second-Class Scout Chuck of the Leadership Corps took off on a trip to a nearby lake with some younger kids.

The group was joined by a couple of non-scouts, one a fifteen-year-old who turned out to be a lousy swimmer.

While everyone else was having fun, this kid was drowning in fourteen feet of water in the middle of the lake. The only person close to him was Chuck, who was forty yards away.

The scoutmaster told me the rest of the story:

"I was on the shore, and I saw the kid go under for the first time. Then I saw Chuck turn back toward the middle of the lake to go after him. I knew for sure I was about to see a double tragedy. I didn't see how Chuck could swim all the way out there and then save both of them.

"I jumped in my canoe, but I knew there was no way I'd get there in time. I just hoped we could pull them off the bottom of the lake and resuscitate them in time to save their lives.

"When Chuck got there, he was immediately pulled under by the struggling kid. A drowning swimmer has tremendous strength. Then I saw them come up again and Chuck had gotten away, but he wouldn't give up. He circled around the kid, talking to him, trying to calm him down. Then he went after him a second time. This time he managed to grab an arm and dragged the kid to shore. I don't know how, but he saved him."

Chuck was hesitant to talk about it, but I persisted until he told me what happened. "When we went under, I hit him in the stomach and he let go of me. I just couldn't let him drown."

"Chuck never had a lifesaving course," said the scoutmaster. "What he knew, he learned from reading the manual. He's dedicated to Scouting. He never thought of the danger. He never thought of his own safety."

I remember from the creed that Boy Scouts are also brave. Somebody ought to tell the kids at Chuck's school that you can't get much groovier than that.

DEARLY DEPARTED IS GLADLY DEPARTED

This is a true story. Believe me.

There was an automobile accident and a woman in her late thirties was killed. A local funeral home agreed to handle her service.

As friends and relatives were settling into their seats in the funeral home's chapel, a bearded man walked in and took a seat in the front row near the casket. He was dressed like Abe Lincoln, wearing a black suit and a tall black hat. The man, as it turned out, was the common-law husband of the deceased.

The service began and the minister decided to bring a full-length, no-holds-barred, fire-and-brimstone message to the mourners. As he bellowed forth, a man and a woman arrived in the chapel quarreling loudly. It was obvious to the funeral home personnel that they had been drinking.

"All I could do," said one employee, "was hope the preacher would quit soon and we could get out of the chapel before there was a ruckus."

Turns out the woman involved in the quarrel was the former common-law wife of Abe Lincoln, who was still sitting down front, and the man with whom she was at odds was her current husband.

The plot thickens.

The preacher had no intention of ending his service quickly. As he continued his message, the mourners became restless and several of them ventured into the hallway outside the chapel to stretch their legs or have a smoke. Meanwhile, the rowdy couple continued bickering in the back.

The preacher finally brought the service to an end and everyone adjourned to the cemetery for burial. As the preacher began his closing prayer at graveside, the funeral director thought to himself, "This thing is finally over. We're going to get out of here without an incident."

He was wrong. Suddenly, Abe Lincoln and his former wife's current husband squared off. They took off their coats and shouted at each other as calmer heads held them apart. Then Abe's former wife decided to get into the act and began to give him a piece of her mind. Before anybody could put out that brush fire, Abe decided he had had enough verbal abuse for one day and hauled off and decked his ex-wife.

"Cold-cocked her," was the description given by one witness.

Finally order was restored, the service was completed, everybody went home, the tent came down, the chairs were folded, the flowers were loaded on the truck and the deceased was buried.

A week later, however, a shooting was reported in town. When police arrived, Abe was firing shotgun blasts into a van occupied by his ex-wife's new husband. The fact that the van was borrowed didn't matter to Abe. He shot it anyway. Police finally subdued him and hauled him away.

All that's left to ponder is whether or not the dear departed will ever be able to rest in peace after all that's taken place since she left us.

DANCING THE NIGHT AWAY

You find these joints when life is a road trip. There in the Holiday Inn in Texarkana, or two blocks down to Shoney's and then hang a right in Rock Hill or Tupelo.

There's a bar and a bandstand, and they pour in off the main road when the darkness catches them tired and lonely. A man peddles industrial lubricants all day and his needs at night are simple: a drink, a dance and then you take your chance.

"Grover and the Groovers" are on the bandstand playing "Proud Mary," the anthem of the just-off-the-interstate roadhouse.

"Beer in a bottle," I shout to the waitress. Grover and the boys are waking the dead for miles around.

"All we got is draft," the waitress shouts back. She's early to middle forties. She outgrew her outfit when Ford was president. Somebody left her and there's the kids to feed and the "Z" she can't afford needs new tires. The story is always the same.

I can't believe they don't have beer in bottles.

"Don't want nobody to get knocked in the head," she explains.

I accept the draft. Grover asks for requests.

"Feelings!" yells a woman from across the room. Grover nods approval. I think, Oh no, not again.

The men are mostly married. Maybe a few clean one-owners, but mostly married. Their wives trust them. The women just came here to dance. They tell themselves that over and over.

Lots of beehives. The aroma of Spray 'n' Set is rampant.

I watch the phenomenon as Grover and the boys launch into "Feelings." The men, who have gathered securely at the bar as a covey, are flushed out toward the tables where the women are sitting, usually two by two.

The procedure is tough on women. Say nobody asks you to dance. Or say a man walks over and asks your friend ("If there was more light in here, he'd have asked me"). Or, worse, the one who asks is wearing a jacket with "Rockwell Power Tools" emblazoned across the back.

It's even tougher for men. I watch one of them — his shirt is a collector's item — give it a try. He takes a pull off his draft, hitches his pants and walks the long mile to where she is sitting. As he stands in front of her, his weight shifts from one foot to the other. She smiles, but her head and the beehive shake, "No."

Years ago I was sitting in such a bar with a friend. He tried. She said no, too.

"Toughest thing in the world is walking over and asking a woman to dance," I philosophized to him later.

"No, it isn't," he said. "It's walking back."

GUTS AT AN EARLY AGE

Larry has a little boy named Joe, who is six years old. When Larry talks about his son, the look in his eyes changes and the love shows through.

Little Joe is a man's kid. He's tough. Women often tell men that the problem with us is that we try to run through too many walls instead of just walking around, but Little Joe would run through a wall if his dad asked him to. There are just some things women don't understand.

Although he's only six, Little Joe joined a Midget League football team with some of the neighborhood kids. Larry told me what happened:

"Joe's the kind of kid most coaches hate to see coming," he said. "He doesn't have any talent yet, he's flat footed and slow as mud, and he weighs only about forty-five pounds. Other kids his age weigh fifty-five to sixty-five pounds. But he's tough."

The first week of practice, Joe had an accident on his bike and had six stitches taken in his leg. "But he never complained," said Larry. "He did all the running and drills. He never missed a practice. He enjoyed the drills that the other kids hated. But the thing he enjoyed most, and the thing he did best, was hitting."

"Hitting" is football talk for tackling, except it's more than that. It's tackling with unusual aggression.

"The coaches decided to put Joe in at middle linebacker. In the first game, although the other team ran us ragged, little Joe made ten individual tackles and assisted with five others. I told him how proud I was of him."

But after the team got trounced again and again, the coaches finally decided that part of the problem was little Joe — he was just too small — so they benched him.

"I was at practice when he came off the field. He tried to tell me what had happened through his sobs. I don't think the coaches knew how hard he had worked. They never knew about his injury, either. It broke the kid's heart, and mine, too, to see him play above his ability and stand and fight when other kids might have given up," said Larry.

"I would tell him that his heart will carry him farther than his legs, that you can't measure desire, that the fastest horse doesn't always win the race, that if he fights hard enough and long enough his reward will come...but in the form of a broken heart?"

I am not a father and by no means an expert, but what I would do is forget the poetic approach. I'd turn in his pads and helmet, tell him I love him and send him out in the back yard to play in the dirt, which is what a six-year-old, bless his little heart, should be doing with his spare time in the first place.

A GAMBLER ON A ROLL

I wandered into a local bar and sat next to a man who was

nursing a drink. There were two quarters sitting by his glass.

"Want to match for a drink?" he asked.

A perfect stranger wants to play a small game of chance. I was hesitant.

"I just want to see if I'm still hot. You see, I'm on an incredible roll. I've just gotten off a plane from the Bahamas where I was up over $20,000 playing blackjack. I want to see if my luck is still holding," he explained.

I told him I'd be glad to buy him a drink if he'd just tell me how to win twenty grand at blackjack. The only time I get lucky playing that game is when I get sleepy and have to go to bed.

"I just sat down at the table at six last Friday afternoon," he began. "I started off with $200. When I woke up Saturday morning, I was up $20,000. The only thing I did was not take a hit if the dealer had six or less showing. It was ten percent knowledge and ninety percent luck.

"On Saturday morning, I realized if I continued playing, I might lose all I had won, so I decided to buy something while I still had some money. I got a security guard from the hotel to go with me, and I went to downtown Nassau and bought a Presidential Rolex watch. Cost me six thousand," he continued.

"I started playing again at six Saturday night. In the first twenty minutes, I was up another $11,000. But by ten I had cooled off and was down to only $12,000, so I decided to take the money and run. The hotel paid for my room, gave me free meals with Dom Perignon and drove me to the airport in their limo."

Counting the $12,000 in cash and the six in a Rolex, he walked away an $18,000 winner.

"It was the most incredible thing that's ever happened to

me. Now, let's match for a drink."

What the heck. We both flipped.

"Same," he said. And they were.

"Once more?" he asked.

I agreed and we flipped again. He won again.

"One more time?"

"I'm already down two drinks," I said, "but let's just go to see how long this streak can last."

We flipped. He called same. I had heads. He had tails.

"Maybe the streak is finally over," I said.

"Maybe," he answered, and I thought I detected a sigh of relief.

REACHING OUT A HELPING HAND

I received a letter in the mail recently which deserves to be shared.

"I don't have much education," began the writer, "but I've got something inside me I want to get out. I thought maybe you could help me."

Not much background is necessary. The man works in a K-Mart. His wife is a nurse. He moved out of the city a few years ago so he could put some cows in a pasture and raise his kids, four of them, on a farm.

"Here I sit, pulling on a longneck beer. I'm not trying to get drunk, just trying to understand. Ten days ago my wife, myself and our four-year-old daughter visited Atlanta to see a doctor that had been recommended to us. The problem was that my little girl has crossing of her eyes. Our oldest daughter had the same problem when she was five or six, so we figured this one had the same thing.

"The first doctor referred us to another and then he sent us to another, and after four doctors, my little girl was finally admitted to the hospital. Just to make sure, they said. Just a few tests. The next day we waited. We waited all day. The tests would come the next day, they said. Finally she was taken down for a brain scan. The machine was down so we waited some more.

"About six on the second day, one of the doctors came and told us that she had a tumor at the base of her brain stem. Because of its location, it is inoperable. The tumor affects her motor functions. Before she was a vivacious little blonde, looking forward to life. Now she drools and stumbles and slurs her speech. She's undergoing radiation therapy, but her prognosis is not good. My only hope is to make these last few months as enjoyable for her as possible.

"But this is not really what I wanted to say to you. I wanted to get across how I feel about those who have helped this family since this tragedy struck. We moved here from the city, and I didn't know the local people had accepted us. But I have never seen such an outpouring of love.

"I didn't know things like this went on anymore. I didn't know there were so many people who still care and love their neighbors. They have brought food. They have helped my wife. They have even contributed money.

"I wish I had the talent of a writer to really get across what is in my heart. I am so moved by how much love and kindness others have shown me, my wife and my little girl that I just want to share it with somebody else. I'm not asking for handouts, but if you see fit to use any of this letter, just tell your readers to look around them. They probably have friends they never knew they had before, friends just waiting for the chance to help them.

"And one other thing. Tell them to love their kids. One day they might not have them anymore. Thanks."

No. Thank you.

— 8 —

What's the Penalty For An Illegal Upchuck?

SPORTS HAS ALWAYS BEEN a great proving ground of character. Kids grow up hearing clichés about the values of sports:

- When the going gets tough, the tough get going.
- Quitters are always losers and losers are always quitters.
- It's not whether you win or lose but how you play the game.
- Show me a good loser and I'll show you a frequent loser.
- It ain't over till it's over.

One of the first sports a kid is exposed to is fishing, since dad is always dragging a son or daughter along to carry the tackle box. As a result of my childhood memories of fishing from the banks of various lakes and rivers, I have always maintained my affection for wetting a line.

Not long ago I was standing along the bank of a creek that runs through one of the golf courses of the magnificent Greenbriar Hotel in White Sulphur Springs, West Virginia. I was there because a man at the pro shop assured me I could catch a huge rainbow trout from that bank. I have never caught a rainbow trout — huge or otherwise. I have watched those television fishing shows where somebody is always landing a big trout, and I've read the magazine articles about techniques, but the closest I've ever been to landing one is in the fish department of the Kroger.

The man at the golf shop rented me a spinning rod and some sort of lure that looked like a roach dressed up for a night out at the disco. "This drives 'em crazy," said the man, who also explained that I could keep any four fish I caught and that the cooks up at the hotel would fillet them for me and serve them for my lunch.

Imagine the thrill: out in the wilds of West Virginia, casting for rainbow trout, and later I would dine on my own tasty catch. Eat your heart out, Gaddabout Gaddis.

The water was so clear that I could actually see the fish swimming around in the creek. They were beautiful and just the right size for eating. I made my first cast and got ready for the tug. Nothing. I cast again. Still nothing. As I was reeling in for my third cast, a trout almost had a head-on collision with my lure but managed to swerve out of the way at the last minute.

About that time, a small boy appeared and began fishing next to me.

"Toss it right in there, Scottie," said the kid's father.

Scottie was dressed in official trout fisherman's garb: floppy hat with flies stuck in it, fishing jacket with lots of pockets and a creel over his shoulder. A creel is what trout fishermen put their fish in. The guy at the pro shop had given me a plastic laundry bag for my catch. I didn't care for Scottie the minute I saw him.

Scottie cast where his dad had advised and almost immediately yelled, "Look, Dad! I've got one." The little brat reeled in a gorgeous rainbow. I reeled in and moved down the bank a little farther.

"Dad," I heard the kid say, "I've got another one!"

"Good going, Scottie," his dad answered.

Get out of my life, Scottie, I thought to myself.

I never did catch a rainbow trout that day. In fact, I didn't catch any fish that day. Not only that, I hung my line in an overhanging tree and lost that funny looking roach lure.

"Look, Dad," said Scottie. "That man has caught a tree." Dad and Scottie had a big laugh. I reeled in my line and started to head back for the pro shop with homicide on my mind.

"Would you like to have these fish Scottie caught?" the dad asked as I was leaving. "We still haven't eaten the ones we caught yesterday."

"No thanks. I hate fish," I said.

Of course, by the time I arrived back at the office, my catch was considerable and never had I enjoyed a finer meal than those rainbows I had pulled from the creek. That's another thing kids learn early about fishing — lying is part of the sport. Consider these standard examples:

QUESTION: So, how were they bitin'?
ANSWER: Had to stand behind a tree to bait our hooks.
TRUTH: The mosquitoes didn't even bother us.

QUESTION: Did you have a guide?
ANSWER: One of the best.
TRUTH: Luckily, the day we got hopelessly lost my five-

99

year-old kid remembered the way back to the dock. I found the bar on my own.

QUESTION: Anybody get sunburned?
ANSWER: Are you kidding me?
TRUTH: I was out of intensive care in no time.

QUESTION: How many did you catch?
ANSWER: Filled up two ice chests.
TRUTH: With beer. The fish fit in my shirt pocket.

QUESTION: What were you fishing for?
ANSWER: Trophy bass.
TRUTH: I'd have been happy with a small frog.

QUESTION: See any snakes?
ANSWER: Big moccasin fell off a tree limb into my boat, but I killed it with the paddle.
TRUTH: A Louisiana pink worm crawled out of the bait box. I made the kid put it back.

QUESTION: So what did you catch?
ANSWER: Largemouths, mostly.
TRUTH: One carp and a turtle.

QUESTION: What did you catch them on?
ANSWER: Top-water plugs.
TRUTH: The carp had a heart attack and floated to the top of the water. My kid caught the turtle and took it home for a pet.

QUESTION: Can't wait to get out there and get at 'em again, huh?
ANSWER: Next chance I get.
TRUTH: I traded my tackle box for two six-packs.

***

When I got older and more sophisticated, my friends urged me to join them in a sport more appropriate for that time in our lives — golf. I later figured out that the people who encouraged me to play golf disliked me very much. It has to be the most frustrating game ever invented.

Because of my history of heart problems, I try not to play more than once a year. In that length of time I usually forget how awful it was the last time and am willing to take another swing.

Golf, I'm convinced, was conceived by real estate developers so they would have an excuse for ruining perfectly good forests and pastures. After the golf courses are completed, these scoundrels further ravage the countryside by building condominiums along the fairways. Rich Republican retirees move into the condos and become even stuffier than they were before.

In fact, stuffiness is probably the no. 1 characteristic of golf. Have you ever listened to the announcers broadcasting the Masters golf tournament? They sound like they're doing the play-by-play for a state funeral. Golf would be more fun if somebody would belch occasionally.

My most recent annual swing at golf came in Myrtle Beach, South Carolina. A companion and I paid a week's salary for green fees, rental clubs, an electric cart and a half-dozen orange golf balls (I could have sworn they were white the last time I played, but maybe that was tennis).

On the first tee my playing partner and I made a small wager, another integral part of the game, and then proceeded to tee off. Unfortunately, my first drive sliced into the backyard of somebody's condominium where a Tupperware party was in progress. I got a free container suitable for serving congealed salads and a free drop off the coffee table.

My second shot, a three wood, caught a tree limb and bounced back toward the Tupperware party, coming to rest on a plate of cheese and crackers the ladies were munching with their white wine. This time I bought six cups and a casserole container to pay for the damages and pitched back into the fairway. I took a twelve on the first hole. My companion went one-up with an eleven.

We both went into the water on the second hole — the water in a swimming pool located behind somebody else's condominium where a woman sat reading a copy of *Cosmopolitan*. My companion removed his tennis shorts and waded into the pool to retrieve our errant shots. The woman went inside and fetched her husband, a very large man, who threatened to call the authorities if we weren't off his property in thirty seconds.

In our haste to leave, we drove the cart over one of the pool chairs, which wouldn't have been all that bad had it not been the one the woman was sitting in at the time. Luckily, the poor woman was unhurt, but her *Cosmo* got caught under one of the cart wheels and we scattered a series on unsightly liver spots for several hundred yards.

I finally shot a sixty-six on the front nine. My companion had a sixty-two and took me for a dollar. We intended to play the back nine, too, but my friend had decided to take his shirt off and catch a few rays. As we made the turn, the head pro requested that we leave the course immediately. We might have resisted, but he made the request while drawing back a four-iron.

Undaunted, we drove to the strip on Myrtle Beach and got in a quick eighteen holes at Jungle Jim's Carpet Golf, where they don't care if you take off your shirt just as long as you don't steal the scoring pencils.

Relieved to get away from the stuffiness of the regular

links, I got my dollar back on the last hole by sinking a long putt that rolled into the monkey's mouth, out through his tail, then under the giraffe's legs, dropping squarely into the cup.

Actually, golf would be a lot more fun if the rules were a little more flexible. For example, I have come up with my own rules guaranteed to add enjoyment to your round:

• THE MILLIGAN RULE — Most golfers know what a mulligan is. That's when you get to hit a second shot off the first tee because your first shot went into the next county. The "milligan" takes that a step further. If you don't like your first shot off any tee, hit another one. If that shot is lousy, too, then hit a "McMilligan," which is a third shot. If that shot is also poor, drive the cart out into the middle of the fairway about 250 yards and drop your ball there. That's called a "Grover McMilligan," named for a famous card cheat who died in a lynching accident.

• MOVING THE BALL IN THE ROUGH — Under my rules, you may not only move your ball in the rough, you also may ignore rough altogether and put your ball back in the fairway ten yards closer to the hole for each form of reptilia spotted while you were in the weeds looking for your ball. A snake and two turtles can make a long hole play much shorter.

• LOST BALL RULE — Let's say you hit your ball into the water and it can't be retrieved. What you do is subtract two strokes from your eventual score on the hole. You deserve it. You just paid three bucks for a brand-new golf ball, and now it sleeps with the fishes.

• SAND RULE — Whose idea was it to put sand on a golf course in the first place? When your ball goes into the sand, remove it as quickly as possible to a nice flat place on the green. That's called a "sandie" in golfing lingo.

- TREE RULE — If you were aiming at a tree and hit it, then you must play the ball as it lies. However, if you were aiming down the middle of the fairway and hit a tree, don't let it ruin your round. Move the ball fifty yards closer to the green for each variety of pine tree you can name.

- TWO-PUTT RULE — If you still aren't in the hole after two putts, pick up your ball and place it in the cup. If your opponent complains, put his head in the hole.

- BEER RULE — At the end of your round, count up the total number of beers you drank during your round and subtract that number from your score. If you had been sober, that's probably what you would have shot in the first place.

***

Golf is not the only game that could benefit from a few adjustments in the rules. Professional tennis, basketball and baseball also could be made more exciting.

In tennis, for example, one of the biggest problems today is players berating the officials. Every time they disagree with a call, they question some linesperson's parentage.

I propose arming each linesperson and the umpire with a big stick, just the kind you would take along on a walk in the woods in case you had to beat a snake. Let's say John McEnroe, one of the most frequent offenders, is playing. He serves, rushes to the net, hits a backhand volley which his opponent returns down the line. The linesperson signals that the ball is in.

"What?" screams McEnroe, turning red in the face. He stomps the ground, breaks his racquet and pulls his hair. Then he calls the linesperson a dirty, rotten so-and-so with everybody in attendance listening. At that point, the linesperson gets out of his or her chair, walks over to McEnroe and bashes him over the head with the stick. A couple of times having a tune played on his noggin will improve his behavior immensely and thereby make the game more enjoyable for the rest of us.

My friend and step-brother Ludlow Porch, a great philosopher, came up with a similar plan to bring baseball more in line with popular tastes.

"Americans love rough contact sports," Ludlow explained, "like football and boxing and hockey and pool."

Pool is a rough contact sport?

"Not the game itself," he said, "but the knife fight that breaks out every night in any decent pool hall certainly is."

So Ludlow has a plan to put more rough stuff into baseball.

"You add two new players. One plays behind the shortstop. That's your left-mugger. Another plays behind second base, and he's your right-mugger. Now, say the batter hits the ball to the third baseman. He throws it to the right-mugger. The runner is not allowed to stop on a base, so he is chased by the right-mugger, who, in order to get the runner out, must knock him to the ground and hit him square in the mouth with the ball and hold him down long enough for the umpire to count to three."

But isn't that terribly unfair to the baserunner, not to mention dangerous?

"There is one other thing," Ludlow said. "The guy who hits the ball gets to carry something with him for protection when he meets a mugger on the basepaths."

And what is that?

"His bat."

The biggest problem with basketball is that all the players have outgrown the game. Guards used to be quick little fellows who could dribble through a church picnic without getting potato salad on the ball. They shot two-handed set shots from the cheap seats and married squatty home-ec majors, and they produced more guards and squatty home-ec majors.

Today guards are so tall they don't even need a ladder to get arrested for peeping into the third floor of the girls' dorm to see if the home-ec majors really have thighs as big as their own.

The big man in basketball used to be any awkward boy over six feet tall who didn't mind being called "Stretch." Today, the big men are what former coach Al McGuire calls "aircraft carriers." You could land on them. They marry girls nobody used to want to dance with and together they produce more "aircraft carriers."

What I propose is legislation to prohibit anyone over six-five from marrying anyone over five-six. That way we won't have to ruin the game for future generations by raising the basket (or, if you're a Democrat, by lowering the floor).

A second way to improve basketball is to do away with the clock. Without a doubt, the "stall," designed to run time off the clock, is the worst thing ever introduced to basketball. It's about as exciting as watching cabbage boil. The rule should be that the first team to score one hundred points wins the game. Clean and simple. And the wives of the losing team have to provide punch and cookies following the game.

***

After my bad experiences with golf, I gave up participatory sports and became a professional spectator. I started with one of the loveliest spectacles of all — the Kentucky Derby.

I reached Louisville, Kentucky, site of "The Derby," after

sixteen hours on an Amtrak train. I could have made it faster in a wheelbarrow but probably wouldn't have had nearly as much fun. The club cars are pretty small in most wheelbarrows. Upon my arrival, my hosts informed me that we did not actually have seats at Churchill Downs. Instead, we were going to leave at six A.M. to attempt to fight off fifty thousand others for a spot in the infield to watch a five o'clock race.

"Will we be able to see any of the Derby from that vantage point?" I asked.

"If you actually wanted to see the race," my host said, "what are you doing in Louisville? You could have stayed home and watched it on television."

So I trekked out to the track at sunrise the next morning and pretended to have a good time until the preliminary races started sometime after lunch. That's when I broke away from my group to try out the new system I had devised for betting and winning on the horses.

My plan was to bet on horses with names that began with an *l* or an *m* or a *g*, which are my initials. That meant that I bet on Lollipop, Milky Way and Gone for Good.

Lollipop couldn't have won on six legs. Milky Way melted in the stretch and Gone for Good is exactly what happened to the two bucks I bet on him.

In the next race I bet on a horse named Liar's Poker. If anybody sees Liar's Poker, tell him to find another line of work. Later I heard two guys talking about a horse that was supposed to be a good mudder. Mudder starts with an *m*, so I bet two dollars on him. Unfortunately, it was a clear day at Churchill Downs and the stupid horse came in last — in the next race.

In desperation I went down next to the track and leaned on the rail, hoping to pick up some tips that way. One of the guys who rides the horses that accompany the thoroughbreds to the gate rode past.

"Hey, fellow, got any good tips today?" I asked him.

"Yeah," he said, "we just painted that rail."

Now I hate horses, too.

***

I finally decided that the best sport for me was good ol' American football. Nothing frilly, no condominiums along the sidelines, just cold beer and fried chicken on a tailgate before the game.

I started with college football and was having a great time until I became disillusioned. I discovered quite by accident that some college football teams were actually cheating. Obviously they never heard another of those childhood clichés: Cheaters never win.

What happened was that this kid in my hometown was being recruited by the University of Florida, a school which has been caught more than once with its hand in the proverbial cookie jar. He received a letter from the head coach and brought it over to Bogator Green's mechanic and body shop for us to see. Here's what the letter said:

> "Dear Prospective Florida Football Recruit:
>
> "Soon you will be deciding where you will be playing college football for the next four years. As head coach at the University of Florida, I thought you might like to know what to expect when you visit with our recruiters and when you visit here on the Florida campus.
>
> "Our recruiters are very nice people and they are very generous. Let's say, for instance, that you really like the new Corvette that one of our

recruiters drives when he visits your home. You might try asking if he would mind if you took the car for a spin. The recruiter might surprise you by saying, 'I really don't need a car like this, so why don't you borrow it?'

"This, of course, would not mean the coach was actually giving you the car, which is against NCAA regulations; it would mean he was lending it to you. Simply remember to leave the keys in the car following your final year of eligibility.

"Since NCAA regulations allow only one official visit to each campus, we want your stay on the Florida campus to be a memorable one. Make certain you do not miss the Florida School of Forestry's famous 'money tree.' On the tree you will find bills of various denominations that always seem to blossom during recruiting season. The bigger bills, incidentally, are toward the top for all you blue-chippers who excel in the vertical leap.

"You may also be asking yourself, If I sign with Florida, how many tickets will I get? We will provide enough tickets so your parents and relatives will be able to see you play. Let's say you received twenty tickets per game. You give your parents one each and your sister and her boyfriend one each. That leaves sixteen tickets. What should you do with them? Why not sell your remaining tickets to a wealthy alumnus? It is against NCAA rules to sell the tickets for more than the price marked on the ticket, but if a wealthy alumnus happens to drop a couple of hundreds out of his pocket during the transaction and you happen to find them after he walks away, is that your fault?

"Some of you might also want to earn money in the off-season. At Florida we offer a complete job placement plan for our student athletes. For example, you might be in charge of making certain the house plants in the head coach's office always have plenty of water. This will teach you how to handle responsibility, as well as earn off-season bucks. This job, incidentally, is currently paying $400 per week.

"You may also want to meet some of the top Florida alumni and boosters. We could arrange for you to meet George Steinbrenner, the wealthy owner of the New York Yankees, at his Bay Harbor Inn in Tampa. If there should be a mix-up at the reservations desk and you are not charged for your three-bedroom suite, leave quietly by the side door so as not to embarrass anyone..

"You may want to know, too, If I sign with Florida, will I be playing for winning teams? We are installing a new system at Florida that should guarantee us many wins. I can't go into details, but it was designed by a loyal Florida alumnus currently working with the CIA.

"Finally, you may be wondering if you are academically qualified for a football scholarship to Florida. Here's a test: How many teams are in the Big Ten? If your answer was ten, no sweat. If it wasn't, we'll think of something.

"See you soon, and go Gators!"

***

I also have a problem with professional football — I can't

understand the terminology that the announcers use. After many Sunday afternoons in front of the tube with dictionary and notepad at hand, I have come up with a guide to modern football lingo which I hope will help others:

• HANG TIME — What time they will be hanging this or that coach for failing to win his division. Sometimes head coaches are hung in effigy. This year they probably will be hung in Denver and New Orleans as well.

• NICKEL BACK — Fifth-round draft choice out of Arkansas State whose agent got him a $150,000-per-year, no-cut contract and he isn't worth a nickel.

• "HI, MOM!" — The most intelligent statement an NFL wide receiver can think of on the spur of the moment when the television camera catches him picking his nose after a long touchdown reception.

• ERIC HIPPLE — What gets in a player's bellybutton after he crawls around on artificial turf for a couple of hours.

• AHMAD RASHAD — Disease a player can get between his toes if he doesn't change his socks often enough.

• TWO-MINUTE WARNING — When a player is caught in a compromising position with a teammate's wife in the teammate's house and the teammate pulls into the driveway unexpectedly. The player has approximately two minutes to get dressed and sneak out the back door before his teammate catches him and breaks his face.

• ILLEGAL CHUCK — Illegally impeding the progress of a receiver named Chuck who is more than five yards down the field.

• ILLEGAL UPCHUCK — Throwing up on the playing surface. Five yard penalty if the surface is grass, fifteen if it is artificial turf.

• ATTACKING UNDER THE COVERAGE — How to

111

make friends with a Dallas Cowboys cheerleader.

• BUMP AND RUN — What to do in case you smash into a Rolls in the parking lot before the game in your 1973 Plymouth Fury.

• 3-4 — How many beers a Pittsburgh Steelers fan has before breakfast on the day of a big game.

• HOWARD COSELL — The end of the horse you never saw when "Mr. Ed" was still on television.

For anyone who doesn't know, the preceding terms apply to American football, not rugby which the English call football and not to that half-breed which the Canadians mistakenly call football.

Several years ago when the National Football League went on strike, American television stations broadcast several Canadian football games to try to satisfy the public's appetite, but I don't think it worked. I was standing in Sonny Bryan's barbecue joint in Dallas, a hotbed of football if ever there was one, when two ol' boys came in talking about a Canadian football game they had seen on TV.

"Frank," the first one said to his buddy, "I believe that was the worst thing I ever saw. I'd just as soon watch a soccer game from Afghanistan."

"Earl," said the other, "I don't think they play soccer in Afghanistan."

"Well, I'd just as soon watch it anyway. When I turned on my set the score in that football game was 14-1. I'm talking about *one*, Frank. How in the hell can you score just one point in a football game?"

"I think it has something to do with not being able to run a punt out of the end zone," said Frank.

"That's another thing," said Earl. "Them end zones are big enough to graze a hundred head of cattle in. And the dad-blame field is 110 yards long. Didn't they read the rule book when they started playing football in Canada?"

"Well, at least it was football," said Frank.

"Wasn't no such a thing," answered Earl. "Listen to me. I been to ever' Cowboys game since we got us a team. I seen Meredith. I seen Staubach. I seen 'em all. And I ain't interested in watching no bunch of castoffs who couldn't play for TCU run around on no oversized football field in some foreign country where all they got is snow and gooses."

"You mean snow and geese," said Frank.

"Them too," said Earl. "And I'll tell you something else. They got strange names for their teams up there. They got a team called the Argonauts. What do you reckon an Argonaut is?"

"I think it's some kind of moose," said Frank. "They got lots of mooses in Canada."

"Mooses?" asked Earl.

"Mooses," answered Frank.

"Let me ask you something, Frank," said Earl. "If gooses is geese, then how come mooses ain't meese?"

"Dang if I know," said Frank. "I don't speak a word of Canadian."

My sentiments, exactly.

— 9 —

Fill 'er Up?
Regular or Harold?

IT'S TOUGH BEING a male chauvinist these days. Talk about something that will build character and develop grit. I can't even joke about it for fear that some woman will do severe harm to my person (body would be a sexist term in that context). The only reason more men aren't being beaten up by women these days is that no matter how far they've come in other areas, most women still can't run very fast and they'll take a double-pump fake every time.

The fact of the matter is that I don't have many chauvinistic attitudes myself, but since some of my friends do, I decided to help them by starting a Male Chauvinist Hotline. Through my newspaper column, I answered questions regarding men's and women's rights. Following are a few of the more helpful selections:

QUESTION: What makes you think you're such an expert on women?

ANSWER: I have been married three times, and I was deeply involved with several other women who auditioned for the part.

QUESTION: Isn't it true that women are more easily frightened than men?

ANSWER: Just because they always go to the restroom in pairs? Of course not.

QUESTION: I work in a steel mill. My foreman says he is going to have to hire some broads. Do I have to put up with that?

ANSWER: Yes, but look on the bright side. Maybe one of your female co-workers will let you have one of her stuffed celery stalks for lunch one day.

QUESTION: My girlfriend is always telling me what great athletes women make. I don't believe that because I still haven't seen a woman who can slam dunk a basketball. How can I overcome such a sexist feeling?

ANSWER: Next time you want your dinner cooked, call Julius Erving.

QUESTION: My wife says I never do anything to make her feel younger. Her birthday is next week. What should I give her?

ANSWER: A six-pack of Oil of Olay.

QUESTION: How many women does it take to replace a lightbulb?

ANSWER: Three. That's one to call her mother for advice on the subject, one to mix the strawberry daiquiris, and one to light the candles when mother doesn't answer.

Despite my vast knowledge of feminine ways, I confess

I've had my share of problems with them, too. I was once married to a young woman who became angry at me for missing a dinner party she was giving for her parents. I missed the dinner because I was playing tennis and the match went three sets and then we had to drink a beer.

The next morning I awoke to find my wife had taken one of the Ginsu knives I had bought for her birthday and cut the strings out of my tennis rackets. I learned my lesson well: I never bought her any more sharp instruments for her birthday.

But that incident was nothing compared to what happened to some of my friends. One fellow's girlfriend discovered he was fooling around with somebody else, so she slipped into his apartment while he was working, took a jar of honey from the refrigerator and poured it all over the kitchen floor. Then she opened the kitchen door and invited in every ant within three counties.

My friend Rigsby probably got it worse than anybody. When his first wife caught him messing around, she went into his closet and cut the ends off all of his ties and one leg off of each pair of pants.

"My second wife topped that," explained Rigsby. "She took all my suits and loaded them into the trash compactor. Take my word for it, a trash compactor adds new meaning to the word wrinkle. Then my third wife scored the coup de grâce. I had a convertible that I kept parked in the garage. She got so mad at me one day that she called a concrete company and had them fill my convertible with cement."

"Well," I said, "it looks like you're doing all right. You must have gotten a sympathetic jury for your divorce case."

"Sympathetic?" said Rigsby. "They came back in after a couple of hours of deliberations and asked the judge for more instruction."

117

"What could they want after two hours?"

"They wanted to know if they could give the death penalty in an alimony case."

I get pretty much the same treatment from my secretary, the lovely Miss Wanda Fribish. Behind every successful man, one can usually find a pleasant, agreeable, supportive secretary. Behind a failure like myself, however, you take what you can get, which is how I came to hire Miss Fribish.

To keep her from pouring glue over the keys of my typewriter or pulling some such feminist prank, I usually buy her off each Christmas by taking her to lunch at the place of her choice. Last year she chose El Flasho's Burrito Barn, famous for its all-you-can-drink frozen margarita special.

We settled in at a table in El Flasho's and ordered our first round of margaritas. After the third round, Miss Fribish started fidgeting and I could tell she had something on her mind. On the fourth margarita, it spewed forth.

"Come here, Four Eyes," she said, wiping the salt off her mustache and grasping me in a hammerlock, a technique she learned in the Militant Feminist Karate, Kung Fu and Secretarial School, of which she is a proud graduate. "There's a few things I want to get straight with you, you little pencil-necked geek."

"Please continue," I gasped, offering myself, as usual, as the open-minded, willing-to-listen employer.

"I'm sick of working for you," she went on. "The pay's lousy, the hours are miserable, and I have to talk to your creepy friends on the phone. Besides that, I'm tired of your constant sexual harassment."

I normally wouldn't argue with a person holding me in a hammerlock, but I asked Miss Fribish what she was referring to.

"You know what I'm talking about, you lecherous leech," she patiently explained. "Every time I walk into your office, I can feel your eyes undressing me."

I assured Miss Fribish that when I stared at her, it had nothing to do with any sexual intentions or desires. I tried to explain that she often startles me with her attire, like the time she came to work wearing a pair of steel-toed combat boots and a camouflage outfit.

"You know perfectly well why I wore that," she said. "Some of the sisters and I were launching a commando raid on an all-male Rotary Club luncheon, and I didn't want to have to go home and change."

After Miss Fribish reminded me, I remembered the incident well. When the cops arrived, they found her with a Rotarian under each arm, ramming their heads together in time to "Camptown Races," which the organization's piano player was performing to open the meeting.

"One more 'doo-da,'" said the investigating officer, "and the two victims might have suffered permanent brain damage."

Recalling the plight of those two Rotarians, I decided it was an opportune time to give Miss Fribish the small raise I had been considering, and I promised never to look at her with anything but business on my mind.

Of course, Miss Fribish's commando unit finally got what they wanted a couple of years ago when the Supreme Court ruled that the Jaycees and other such groups could not exclude women from their memberships.

Shortly afterwards, I received a call from my old friend Gilbert, who had a novel idea. "Listen to this," he said excitedly. "I'm going to start a club that will be for men only."

"Listen, Gilbert," I said, "you obviously haven't been keeping up with the news. You can't exclude women from clubs anymore."

"No," he argued, "you don't understand. I'm not going to exclude them. I'm just going to start a club that they won't want to belong to. We'll do only the things they don't like. We won't say we're for men only, but as soon as any woman joins she'll be so disgusted that she'll quit. It's a great plan!"

I asked what sort of disgusting and appalling things the members of Gilbert's club would do.

"Just the usual stuff we used to do in the old days," he said. "First of all, we're not going to serve white wine in the bar. That'll cut out two-thirds of the women who might want to be members. Then we're going to drink a lot of beer and belch and fart whenever we feel like it, and we're going to smoke big cigars and blow smoke all over the room. Women hate cigar smoke. And finally, we'll tell all the sexist jokes we used to, like the one about why God created women in the first place."

I asked Gilbert what he intended to name his new club, but he didn't get to tell me.

"I don't have time to talk anymore right now. My wife is having the girls over for a Tupperware party, and if I don't have this house cleaned up by six, she'll kill me."

Admission to previously all-men's organizations was just one of many equal opportunity advancements women have made in recent years. In fact, I can't think of any place between here and outer space where they're not.

Just the other day I stopped into a service station and a woman attendant came out. She seemed quite capable of handling her job and opened with the standard dialogue, except for a small change.

"Fill him up?" she asked.

"Please," I said.

"Regular or Harold?"

"Harold? What happened to Ethyl?"

"She's running for Congress."

I was watching television and a female evangelist came on asking for donations. "This broadcast is run on faith alone," she said. "Send us what you can, we'll take a check or money order, and the Lord will bless you. She told me so Herself."

Next day I walked into a hardware store and there was a woman behind the counter.

"I'd like a garden hose," I said.

"What shade?" she asked.

"I'm not certain," I replied, somewhat taken aback.

"So what color is your lawn?" she continued.

"Green."

"Then I'd suggest something in a soft pastel," she said, "either a melon or perhaps this delightful pink."

I also asked if she knew where I could pick up a used winch.

"Try the bus station about midnight," she replied.

***

One of the few remaining places where men can still be left alone with other men is the old-fashioned barber shop. These are the places that kept their names — the Sportsman Barber Shop, or Haynie's Barber Shop — when others became "styling salons." A man can be as sexist as he wants in such a setting.

"Heard about the two young bulls that met at the fence?" asked my barber, who always has an off-color joke. "One bull says it's great where he is. Plenty of grass to graze on,

121

lots of shade trees around and plenty of heifers to keep him company. He says it's just like heaven on his side of the fence, and he asks the other young bull what it's like on his side.

"The other bull says it's awful. There's not much grass, no trees to stand under when it gets hot and there aren't any heifers at all. He says the only company he's got is an old washed-up steer and all he wants to do is talk about his operation."

My barber also trims my mustache, which qualifies me for another story.

"I got a friend," he says, "who grew himself one of these long, handlebar mustaches. Fellow asked him, 'Don't that mustache bother the women when they kiss you?' My friend said, 'Not a bit. They don't mind going through a little briar patch to get to a picnic.'"

The barber finished my trim and slapped the back of my neck with some cologne. "You need a little of this boy-dog smell," he said.

Yeah, I reckon I do. Don't we all?

***

With the possible exception of the old-fashioned barber shop, women are gaining equality with men in all areas. But lest there be any confusion, I should point out that women themselves are not equal in all respects. As one who has traveled and researched across this great country of ours, I must confess that there are considerable inequities between Northern women and Southern women.

First, there is the matter of yankee women not shaving their legs. This, according to the famous Southern author Homer Southwell, is a custom that began in Buffalo, New York, during the Great Snow Storm of '26. Women found that by not shaving their legs they were afforded natural protection against the snow and cold, and so the entire female population of Buffalo went hairy-legged that winter.

This led, incidentally, to a dramatic fall in the birth rate in Buffalo and also led to the popular folk song, "Buffalo Girls, Won't You Come Out Tonight (And Graze by the Light of the Moon)?"

Most Southern women, of course, wouldn't be caught dead without shaved legs — even big, fat, ugly Southern women who bark at the moon and run rabbits.

Southern women also make better cooks than Northern women. There are even women left in the South who will arise early in the morning and cook their men hot biscuits. Not "whomp biscuits," where you whomp the can on the side of the table, but real biscuits as the Lord intended man to have.

Northern women make good cooks if you like to eat things that still have their heads and eyes, cooked in a big pot with carrots and asparagus and other houseplants.

Southern women aren't as mean as Northern women. Both bear watching closely, mind you, but a Southern woman usually will forgive you two or three times more than a Northern woman before she pulls a knife on you.

Most importantly, Southern women know how to scrunch better. Scrunch is nothing dirty. It's where on a cold night you scrunch up together in order to get cozy and warm. Southern women can flat scrunch. I tried once to scrunch with a yankee girl, but she hadn't shaved her legs and it was like trying to cuddle with a hundred-pound Brillo pad.

So I admit it — even though I'm pretty much an expert on women and certainly open-minded to a new order, I've had my share of trouble with them. But who hasn't? John Wayne had about as many run-ins with them in real life as he did on the silver screen. Heck, even the president of the United States has trouble with women.

I read just the other day where Ronald Reagan and a group of his advisers had a midnight session trying to come up with a plan to bridge the president's gender gap.

"Criminy," said the President, "no matter what I do or say, I can't seem to make America's women happy."

The room was quiet as the President paced. Suddenly he stopped and said, "I think I've got it! Why don't we send every woman in America a big bouquet of flowers with a nice little card attached?"

"Not a bad idea, Mr. President," said one of the advisers. "What would the card say?"

"Something very sweet and tender," said the President. "Women are pushovers for flowers and sweet, tender cards. It could say, 'Roses are red, daisies are yellow, your loving President is a really sweet fellow.'"

"I don't think it would fly," said another adviser. "Women would think you were just trying to buy them off with flowers."

"How about candy then?" asked the President. "Once Mrs. Reagan got very mad at me for talking to a visiting emissary's wife too long at a party, so the next day I bought her a big box of candy and she forgave me."

"Same problem," said the disagreeing aide. "The days when you could woo an American woman with candy and flowers are over."

"Fur stoles are even out of the question?" asked the President.

"You'd lose the conservationist vote if you did that," said another presidential confidant.

The President thought some more. "I think I have it this time," he said. "Whenever candy or flowers or a new fur

124

doesn't work with Mrs. Reagan, I always take her out to a nice restaurant. What if I took all the American women out for dinner? We could go to a real nice place and have champagne, and they could order anything on the menu they wanted. Maybe afterwards, we could go some place romantic for a glass of cognac."

"Now you're really getting some place," another aide spoke up. "You could make it a very intimate evening. Just you and a few million American women."

"It would be very charming," said the President. "I would look into their eyes and tell them how beautiful they all were this evening, and we could have strolling violins to play 'Moonlight Becomes You' to increase the romantic effect."

The adviser who earlier had been against flowers and candy lit a cigarette, blew a puff of smoke and asked, "How long would it take to put something like this together? We're running out of time, you know."

"I don't think it would take too long," said the President. "Of course, we would have to wait long enough for all the women in America to have their hair done and maybe buy a new dress for the occasion."

"I know the maitre d' at Tiberio's," said another aide. "I could find out when he could take a party of several million."

The plan was put into place. The President would phone each woman to be invited and ask her to a quiet dinner with him, "so we can get to know each other a little better." The President would wear his best tux and dash on a little Paco Rabanne cologne, and before the evening was over, the women of America would be eating out of his hand.

Just then Mrs. Reagan came down from the presidential bedroom in her nightgown. "Isn't it time you came to bed?" she asked the President. "My feet are cold."

"Not now, honey," he said. "We're holding man talks."

***

It's been said before, but I agree that bucket seats may have done more to separate men and women than the Baptist church. Back when cars and trucks were equipped with bench seats, women cuddled up next to their men so that sometimes you couldn't tell who was driving.

My boyhood friend and idol, Weyman C. Wannamaker, Jr., a great American, once nearly totaled his 1957 red Chevrolet while out on a date with Kathy Sue Loudermilk. They were driving along a back road looking for a place to stop and discuss one of Weyman's favorite philosophical questions — Is wrestling fake? — when Kathy Sue inched her way over to him. She kept inching, as a matter of fact, until she was slap dab in his lap behind the wheel. Then she proceeded to kiss him squarely on the mouth in a most passionate fashion, which was the only way she knew how.

By the time Weyman managed to bring the '57 Chevy to a halt, he had run over two road signs, three possums and Curtis "Fruit Jar" Hainey, the town drunk. The road signs were demolished, two of the three possums passed away and "Fruit Jar" swore off drinking for an hour.

The man who invented bucket seats obviously never dated Kathy Sue.

There's an old story which says it best:

A man and his wife are riding along and his wife spots a younger couple huddled close together in another car.

"We used to do that twenty-five years ago, honey," she says to her husband. "Why did we stop?"

"Don't ask me," he replies. "I haven't moved."

That's sort of how I feel about the women's movement in general — I haven't moved.

— 10 —

Profiles In
Gray Grit

A S AN ONLY CHILD in a traditional Southern family, I grew up around adults. Not just my parents, but grandparents and uncles and aunts as well. It was an extended family long before anyone decided to call it that.

While they sat on the front porch rocking and shelling peas and telling tales, I picked beggar lice off my pants legs and listened closely. That was probably the best education I ever received, and as I look back on it now from the perspective of near-middle age, I realize there was more wisdom on that porch than I ever imagined.

Listen to a few of these stories of senior citizens and you'll see what I mean.

A PRIVATE WAR ON HUNGER

My grandmother, Willie Word, declared her own war on

hunger years before it became the international issue that it is today. "Every stray dog and cat in the county seems to wind up here," she used to say. It was easy to figure out why. Every stray dog and cat in the county had gotten the word that when all else failed, you always could get a handout at Willie Word's house.

My grandmother also made certain that birds around her yard never went hungry, and when my grandfather complained that the worms had gotten to his tomatoes, she would say, "Even worms have to have something to eat, you know."

She fed her family well, too, of course. My favorite from her table was pork chops. Biting through the flaky crust and succulent meat remains my taste buds' unanimous choice as childhood's best culinary memory. I was an admitted glutton when it came to Mama Willie's pork chops. She always cooked two each for every member of the family, but I always managed to get three.

"Want my last pork chop?" she inevitably asked me, and I inevitably accepted.

One afternoon as I was walking home from a friend's house, I spotted an old man, a tramp, I supposed, lying on the front steps of the Baptist church across the street from where we lived. When I got inside, I told Mama Willie about him.

"He's probably hungry," said my grandmother, who promptly went across the street and fetched him.

He was hungry. You could see it in his eyes as he watched Mama Willie prepare dinner, to which she had invited him. A pork chop dinner. I counted heads and pork chops as we prepared to deliver the blessing. There were five people and only eight pork chops. I was immediately concerned about my usual three.

Mama Willie passed out the pork chops. She placed two on my plate, two on my mother's plate and two on my grandfather's plate. Somebody, I reasoned, is going to miss out on a marvelous pork chop dinner if this trend continues. Then my grandmother gave the ragged old man the other two chops, denying herself any meat that night.

Where, I wondered, is my usual third chop coming from? I ate my first one in a hurry. As I started on my second, I noticed my grandmother staring at me. I looked down at the second pork chop. I looked back at Mama Willie. She motioned her head toward the tramp, who had gone through his two chops in record time and was now attacking the bones. I knew what she wanted me to do.

I had to spit out the words. "Would you like my last pork chop?"

"I'd be much obliged," he said.

I looked back at my grandmother. She was smiling at me.

I haven't sent any money to help the starving people in Ethiopia yet, but I think I will. The memory of that smile demands it.

STILL A FLAME IN THE FIREPLACE

The Atlanta Braves were playing the Toronto Blue Jays in a spring training game in West Palm Beach, Florida. Three or four thousand of us sat blissfully in the sun and watched.

There was more to watch than just the game, however. For instance, there was the girl, a young blonde thing. She wore high heels and tight white pants that came to a few inches below her knees. Had we been hit by high water, she would have been prepared. Call her "The Walker."

She sat for an inning before she started strutting about the stands. To quote William Price Fox, when she moved, the motion in her high-water britches looked like two bob-cats fighting in a croker sack.

When I wasn't watching The Walker, I was watching the old men. What better way to while away a retirement after-noon than to sit and warm yourself over a leisurely baseball game that really doesn't count anyway? If and when I become an old man, I want to come to these games and sit with others my age. I'll probably say a lot of outrageous things. Old men can get away with such as that.

The kids today idolize the current players and go for their autographs like a hound on a good scent. Their heroes still wear the uniform. We middle-agers are losing our heroes in a hurry. Pete Rose and Phil Niekro are still around, but how can I get excited about Dennis Lamp when Sandy Koufax is still fresh on my mind? The old men have their memories, too, and you can hear them in the stands still praising Williams, DiMaggio, Gehrig and even Ruth.

"Now, those were ballplayers," the old men say. "You never saw those guys sitting out a game with a hangnail or a little cold."

There were probably eight of them, the old men, sitting together near me. They sat through the last innings like crows perched on a powerline, silent and staring. When the game was over, they moved slowly out to the aisle. Two needed assistance in walking. They were held on each side by the steadier hands of their companions.

When they reached the walkway out of the stadium, they said their goodbyes. A friend next to me observed, "They seem very sincere about saying goodbye. I guess when you get to be that age, you never know how many empty seats will be on your row tomorrow."

At precisely that moment, The Walker came by. The old men looked at the curves she was throwing, and one smiled at his friend and gave him a knowing wink.

Yeah, they're all getting on, I thought to myself. But bless their hearts, with apologies to Charlie Dressen, they ain't dead yet.

NEW TRICKS FOR AN OLD DOG

My friend Milton is sixty-six. He looks sixty-six. He's been around, Milton has. He was a newspaper copy boy once. He was in the Army. He has seen the world. He has seen this country, all of it, twice — both times from the window of a Greyhound bus.

His first trip was in 1966. It cost him $99 for an unlimited travel ticket, and he used it. New York. Chicago. Seattle. Los Angeles. Back home to Atlanta.

"I mooched off relatives whenever possible," Milton told me. "Other times I'd see a town I liked, get off the bus and stay a couple of days. If it turned out I didn't like the town, I'd grab the next bus out."

Several years ago, Milton took the grand tour again. This time it cost him $159. "I did thirty states and probably one hundred cities," he said. "You get used to the bus. Last time I checked, I still had my spine."

On Milton's first trip, one of his stops was Iowa City, where he walked the campus of the University of Iowa. "I was just walking around looking, waiting for another bus. But something about that campus struck me. It was winter. I looked up at all those towers of learning. I studied all the statuary, and I got an inspiration. I even said a prayer about it. I was determined to get back into college, even at my age."

Almost two decades later, he did it. The Georgia legislature passed a bill granting free tuition to anyone over sixty-two who wanted to attend college.

"It was a dream come true," said Milton. "I really just wanted to see if I could do the work. I didn't know if my brain cells had deteriorated to the point where I couldn't retain anything. I haven't done a lot to prolong them, you know. I've done some riotous living, and I've knocked around half the world on planes and buses and trains, and I've been hit in the head a lot with baseballs. But I'm amazed at what I'm learning. I never knew I was so stupid before."

Milton, of course, isn't stupid at all. He's wise even beyond his years. Old dog Milton is learning new tricks. Don't get old, he advises, just get busy.

"I feel like Alice in Wonderland. I'm in my third childhood. Now, all I want to do is live long enough to graduate."

Any man who can survive two bus trips around this country is a good bet to live through four years of college. Give 'em hell, Milton.

A SOLDIER FOR LIFE

Major Harvey Banks of the Salvation Army retired from active duty way back in the late 1930's. His health was failing, and he was well into his sixties anyway. He tried taking it easy for awhile. Maybe for the first couple of days. But Major Harvey Banks wasn't one to sit still if somebody could use his help.

He visited jails and prisons and sang songs and played music for the inmates. He tried to convince them that his God was theirs, too. He got involved with caring for unwed mothers, and he worked tirelessly in welfare and disaster relief.

"The only difference between Major Banks when he was

retired and Major Banks when he was active," a friend of his told me, "was that after he retired, they put an R at the end of his name."

You see these people who work for the Salvation Army and you wonder about them. What prompts a person to spend his or her life wearing that silly uniform, standing on a street corner tooting a horn or ringing a bell? It's certainly not the money. The base pay for a married Salvation Army officer is approximately $150 a week. If you've got forty-five years in and you're married, you pull in a cool $175 or so a week. Single officers get about sixty percent of those figures.

"We do get our housing," said one member of the Army.

After his retirement, such as it was, Major Banks received a small pension, and his working daughter helped him make ends meet. An old friend said of him, "He lived on faith. The extra energy God gave him, he used in the interest of other people."

Major Banks was born in 1873 in Ontario, Canada. The Salvation Army had been started in London in 1865. It came to this country when Major Banks was six years old. Thirteen years later he joined.

In August of 1982 in an Atlanta, Georgia, nursing home, more than forty years after he had retired from "active duty" due to health reasons, Major Harvey C. Banks died. He was 109.

"He was just as lively as ever, still had a great sense of humor, still had a twinkle in his eyes, still loved to sing and listen to music," said another friend at the Salvation Army headquarters.

There was no long period of suffering for Major Banks. His illness and his subsequent death came quickly. He was the oldest living Salvation Army officer in the world, a man who first gave one life to the assistance of the lost and failing, and then turned around and gave another.

The good die young, they say. Not always, thank God. Not always.

CAMPAIGNING FOR THE LORD

The first time I met Ottis "Smokey" Bailey, he was standing on a corner of Peachtree Street in downtown Atlanta handing out Bibles. Smokey holds that everybody ought to own at least one.

"I don't care what kind of misery you got," Smokey says, "the Book can set you free."

Smokey was doubling as a janitor in an apartment house at the time. He had one room in the basement, and that's where he kept his stacks of Bibles he gave away to anybody who would take one from him. "People are always giving me Bibles to give away," he said, "but I don't never take one from nobody unless they got an extra. If you ever get without a Bible, you're lookin' at the devil right in his eyeballs."

Smokey and I eventually sort of teamed up in his handing-out-Bibles venture. He was the brains and the legs of the operation. I took over the financial and public relations parts. First I wrote a newspaper column about him, asking for spare Bibles. They came in by the truckloads. "I made sure that everybody who sent one in had an extra," I assured Smokey. He seemed relieved.

Later, the management company at the apartment house decided that Smokey was handing out Bibles when he should have been replacing screens, so they put him and his Bibles out on the street. That's when I got involved in the financial end of our business: I gave Smokey twenty dollars.

He's still handing out Bibles, and he'll preach anytime anybody will listen. And I still pass him a twenty
occasionally.

"You know, things been tough on me since my mama
died back in '78." Smokey doesn't need to remind me, but
he always does just the same.

After a considerable absence, Smokey reappeared in my
office just the other day. Outside the streets were flooded
with an April Atlanta monsoon.

"You lookin' well," Smokey said.

"You, too," I answered. "How's it going with the Bibles?"

"Couldn't be better," he said, "but I'm having a little
trouble at the hotel where I'm living."

"Rent trouble?"

"Yeah. I could use about thirty," he said. Inflation, I
reasoned. I asked Smokey if he could come back later since I
was out of cash.

"Could you just give me a check now, brother? It's doing
some powerful raining out there."

Try that line the next time you visit your banker for a loan.

I wrote the check. Smokey blessed me a couple of times
and headed for the door. I looked out my office window a
few minutes later and saw him walking down the sidewalk,
bound for the nearest bank, I suppose. At that very
moment, the sun peeked out from behind the clouds for the
first time in days.

SERVICE THE WAY IT OUGHT TO BE

David Poole and his brother Robert opened their little
garage back in the sixties. They were tired of getting somebody else's grease under their fingernails, so they decided
to give it a shot on their own. Working a mechanic's flat rate

for a greedy dealer can be a going-nowhere treadmill.

For a time it was a good life and a good living for the Poole brothers. They are good, honest mechanics, and they aren't interested in ripping off their customers.

"They've been servicing my cars about as long as I've been driving," a customer told me. "If everybody operated the same way they do, this would be a better world to live in."

A couple of honest, hard-working mechanics satisfying their customers. What a nice little scenario in today's grab-what-you-can scheme of things. Only this story doesn't have a happy ending. A couple of years ago, the break-ins started.

"Had five or six in one year," David Poole said. "We figured we knew who was doing most of it, but we couldn't prove nothing. Police said we'd have to catch him with the goods. It was this little boy, about sixteen. He cleaned us out one time. I mean, he took everything we had, including an old wood step stool and even the nozzles off the air hoses."

The burglaries continued, so the Poole brothers started taking their tools home with them. "Then somebody came in one night and stole all our antifreeze," David said. "Finally we just decided we'd had enough."

After more than twenty years in business, the Poole brothers gave up, victims of urban crime, victims of a judicial system that couldn't stop a two-bit kid burglar from robbing a couple of hardworking, grown men.

"I'm sixty-one," said David Poole. "They've taken things we can't afford to replace now, and I don't feel like starting over anyway. So we just closed for good."

To show the Pooles how much they were appreciated, many of their customers got together and gave them a surprise party at the garage just before it closed. "That was really something," said David Poole, choking on the emotion.

"You know what worries me most about closing?" he asked. "It's the older ladies who have been coming in here ever since we started in business. They don't know a thing about what's wrong with their cars, or what needs to be done. I don't know where they'll go now. I just hope nobody takes advantage of them."

Me, too, David. But I wouldn't bet the nozzle off an air hose that somebody won't.

A WEAK BODY BUT A STRONG WILL

The old man was born in 1888. That's five wars ago, from the Spanish-American to Vietnam. Think of the changes in his lifetime, from horse and buggy to men walking on the moon.

He farmed nearly all his life. Even as he reached the age where he couldn't farm on a large scale anymore, he still maintained his garden.

One of his grandchildren was saying, "I can remember twenty years ago when my mother used to say, 'We've got to go visit Grandpa and Grandma. They won't be around much longer.' That was two decades ago, and they were both in their seventies then."

The grandchildren and great-grandchildren loved the old man. He handed out quarters every time they drove to the country to visit with him, and he obviously took pride in seeing his children's children frolic on the good earth.

He had white hair and wore thin, wire-rimmed glasses until he was well into his nineties. Then he had the cataracts removed and didn't need his glasses anymore. When he took the test to get his driver's license renewed a couple of years ago, his eyesight was nearly perfect.

He had been married to the same woman for more than seventy years. She doted on him. She took care of him. The kids used to wonder what would become of Grandpa if anything ever happened to Grandma.

It came on her slowly. Senility creeps in at first, but then it gains momentum and devours its victim. She started to forget little things. Then she couldn't remember what day it was, who had come to visit last week, where she had put things in the kitchen. When she reached the state where Grandpa could no longer care for her, the kids tried hiring a housekeeper, but Grandma couldn't understand why there was a strange woman in her house and once chased away the housekeeper with a broom.

Without his wife to tend his needs as she had done for most of his life, the old man's health began to deteriorate, too. Just like that. The kids decided their only recourse was to put the couple in a nursing home. In some instances, nursing homes serve a good purpose, I suppose. Neglected and lonely old people are able to get the care they need and are able to have companions.

But sometimes when old people are uprooted, it doesn't work so well. Their roots run too deeply into their home places to pull them away. I remember when my own grandfather died. My grandmother, although she was in ill health herself, couldn't be budged out of the tiny house she had shared with the man she loved.

The old man didn't take to the nursing home. His wife reached the point where she didn't know who he was anymore. The children of four generations visited when they could, but they always found the old man lonely and depressed.

138

"Every time one of us would go to visit him," one of the grandchildren recalled, "he would beg us to bring him a gun. He'd say, 'Let me get this thing over with now.'"

The old man stopped eating. He brooded and cried. He begged to die. Without his wife and away from his home and garden and his dog, he saw no reason to live. They found him in bed one morning not long ago. He had died in his sleep. He was ninety-five.

"He just willed himself to death," said the grandchild. "I guess it was a blessing that he was able to do that."

Medical science has developed all sorts of means to keep people alive, but maybe sometimes it is better to die than to live on beyond your time. The old man was able to make that choice on his own. Maybe that is a blessing, rest his weary soul.

HONEST, MOM, IT'S NO TROUBLE

It's the same story every year at Christmas.

"Son," says my mother, "you don't have to get me anything for Christmas this year."

And I say, "I know that, Mother, but I want to get you something for Christmas."

"Well, I just don't want to be any trouble."

"It won't be any trouble, Mother. That's part of the enjoyment of Christmas, buying gifts."

"There's just no reason to waste your money on me, son."

"Buying you a Christmas present isn't exactly wasting my money," I argue.

"But there's really nothing I need."

"There must be something you need or want."

"You gave me pajamas last year. I have plenty of pajamas."

"So how about house shoes, the fluffy kind?"

"I have a closet full of house shoes already," she says.

"How about a nice nightgown?"

"I'll never use all the nightgowns I have now. Why don't you just take the money you would have spent on me and buy yourself something nice? Do you have a warm coat?"

"Yes, Mother. Three of 'em."

"How about sweaters?"

"I could start my own line of sweaters, I have so many."

"How about a hat?"

"I don't wear hats."

"Well, how do you keep your head warm?"

"My head doesn't get cold."

"You need a hat in the winter. You might catch a cold if you don't wear a hat."

"This is ridiculous. We're supposed to be talking about what I'm going to get you for Christmas."

"What could you get me? I never go anywhere anymore."

"How about a jacuzzi?"

"A what?"

"You'd love it. A jacuzzi is a tub that you fill with hot water, and there are all these jets shooting out water. You sit in there and it's very relaxing. It would be great for your arthritis."

"I never heard of such a thing," she parries.

"What we could do is knock out a wall and extend the bathroom and put the jacuzzi there."

"I don't want a bunch of carpenters sawing and hammering and tracking mud into the house. Don't get me a bacuzzi."

"Jacuzzi."

"However you say it, I don't want it."

"I know there must be something you'd like to have for

Christmas," I persist.

"OK. What I really would like is a pantsuit to wear when I go to the doctor."

"Great. Why didn't you say that in the first place?"

"I didn't want to be a bother."

"It's no bother. What size?"

"Sixteen. Don't let 'em sell you a fourteen, because that's too small."

"What color?"

"Any color, except red."

"Why not red?"

"I'm too old to wear red."

"OK, one non-red pantsuit. Anything else?"

"That's plenty, son. I don't want to be a bother to you."

The pantsuit I bought my mother is blue. It was no bother whatsoever.

— 11 —

Ugly Goes Clear
To the Bone

A MERICA AND MOST of the civilized world has a
fascination with health and beauty. When was the last
time you saw a billboard or a television commercial featuring a fat, ugly person? For those of us not blessed with an
attractive countenance, these can be very trying times.

I've had this problem for years. In fact, when I was born
they called in a vet. My mother was caught two days later in
the nursery trying to switch my ID bracelet with that of
another child. As I was growing up, she tried the old trick of
tying a pork chop around my neck so the dogs would play
with me. The dogs preferred to dig for turnips in the garden
instead.

When my sight started failing in grammar school and I
had to get glasses, that didn't help my looks much either.
My classmates always called me "D.U." That stood for
"double ugly."

"Beauty is only skin deep," I would argue.

"Yeah," they would reply, "but ugly goes clear to the bone."

In the seventh grade we had a Halloween masquerade party at school. The scariest costumes were awarded prizes. The kid who placed first went as me.

Finally in high school my looks became an asset. I was asked to join the Future Farmers of America because they needed a scarecrow for the Spring Corn Festival.

In college everybody went to the beach during spring break, but I was afraid to be seen with my shirt off. So I joined a health spa and asked the instructor what I could do to build up my muscles.

"You want my honest opinion?" he asked.

"Give it to me straight," I said.

"You're wasting your time. It would take you six months just to get into shape to take your 'before' picture."

Not long ago I was showing a friend some of my childhood pictures. "You looked like that?" the friend said.

"That's the way I looked."

"Well, let me ask you something. Did any of your mother's children live?"

***

When the graze craze hit in the late 1960's, the favorite war cry of the health food set was, "You are what you eat." If that were so, I would have been a stick of bologna by the time I was ten. Ugly bologna.

"What's for lunch today?" I would ask my mother.

"Bologna sandwiches," she inevitably would reply.

After six years of the same dialogue, I finally stopped asking. And if I complained, my mother made it into an international incident.

"This stuff makes me want to throw up," I would argue.

"How can you say that with all the starving children in China?" she would counter.

"Name one and we'll send him some of this bologna."

"There's nothing wrong with bologna," she would say. "It's nutritious, it's a bargain and it sticks to your ribs."

What good are fat ribs unless you're a side of barbecue? I always wished it would stick to the roof of my mouth so I wouldn't have to swallow any more of it.

One day while eating yet another bologna sandwich, it occurred to me to ask, "Just what is bologna?"

A hush fell across the room. You would have thought I had asked for an explanation of sexual reproduction. "Well, son," stammered my mother, looking for a way out, "you're not old enough to be asking about such things. Just hush up and eat your bologna."

I don't know if my mother really ever knew what was in bologna, because I still don't know myself. I'm almost afraid to find out for fear that it's something awful. All I know for sure is that I ate a horsecart full of it in my youth. (Why did I say horsecart?)

As I look back on it now, I realize that I learned a great deal from eating all that bologna. I'm sure it has made me a better person. While other kids brought ham sandwiches to school, I ate bologna and learned humility and courage. Believe me, it takes courage to eat that stuff day after day.

But eating bologna, as distasteful as it was, didn't compare to the trauma of being forced to try liver. I knew what it was, and I didn't want any part of it.

"Just try it with a little onion and pepper," said my mother. "You'll find that it's pretty good."

I would have put Forty Mule Team Borax on it if she had let me — anything to kill the taste.

Years later I devised a plan to eradicate crime in America,

and liver formed the guts of the plan. (Why did I say guts?) My unique plan called for crime to be punishable not only by a prison term, but also by being made to eat a food befitting the crime.

For example, a person convicted of first-degree murder would be sentenced to life in prison with nothing to eat except liver three times a day. Manslaughter would get you twenty years of liver, only with onions. Armed robbery would be five to ten of macaroni and cheese, the kind they used to serve in the school cafeteria. Talk about sticking to the roof of your mouth . . . Kidnappers could look forward to ten years of Brussels sprouts, embezzlers to ten years of pork and beans straight from the can and a conviction for fraud would net a sentence of ten years of nothing but Jello — with bits of bologna inside.

Is your kid a wimp or a troublemaker? Does he hang out with punk rockers and whine about everything? Fill him up to his pierced ears with bologna and liver and you'll see an immediate improvement in his character.

It's time to get back to basics, America. Stand up and be counted.

***

Growing up eating bologna and liver may have helped my character, but it didn't do a thing to improve my looks. I still scared cats. But leaving home and not eating bologna and liver didn't seem to help either.

"Gee, I didn't know you'd been in a wreck," people used to say. I hadn't.

Part of the reason for my ongoing uglies may have been my bad eating, drinking and smoking habits. Apparently I was not alone, however, since most people who live by themselves tend to have bad eating habits, I've read. Therefore, in my endless effort to help my fellow Americans, several years ago I developed "The Grizzard Diet for Single Non-Cookers Who Are in a Hurry."

The staples of this revolutionary diet are Maalox (the family-sized bottle), cold tuna salad sandwiches from vending machines, pizza to go and large quantities of alcohol. Of course, you are offered a number of choices to avoid monotony. For example, here's a typical day on "The Grizzard Diet for SN-CWAIAH":

BREAKFAST — Order out for pizza, preferably pepperoni and scrambled eggs. If you can't find anything open at that time of day, eat the cole slaw left over from the night before's Kentucky Fried Chicken dinner.

LUNCH — Rolaids and a large Pepsi.

AFTERNOON SNACK — Maalox and a pint of chocolate milk.

DINNER — Go to a bar and drink yourself silly. Then ask the bartender for a bowl full of olives and maraschino cherries.

LATE-NIGHT SNACK — Call a married friend and ask if they had anything left over from dinner.

The advantage of this diet is that all of the meals are interchangeable. The disadvantage is that after about three months, you look like a prisoner of war; this diet will either kill you or make you tough (see earlier reference to, "When the going gets tough, the tough get going"). After six months friends assume you have anorexia nervosa and feel sorry for you. A single female friend of mine who adhered to this diet for several months was very nearly killed in an accident at a fast-food restaurant. A nearsighted cleaning woman mistook her for a mop and had done half the kitchen floor with the girl's head before she realized the

147

mop was making gurgling sounds when it was raised out of the bucket.

I also lost too much weight on the "Single Non-Cookers Who Are in a Hurry" diet and had to visit weight-gaining expert Cordie Mae Poovey, an old acquaintance from my school days, to get help. When Cordie Mae was eleven, she was already a herd. She once hijacked the local ice cream wagon and ate nine sundaes and seventeen Eskimo Pies before releasing the driver, who was unharmed except for the black eye Cordie Mae gave him when he initially refused to tell her where he kept the chocolate syrup and whipped cream.

Cordie Mae, currently employed in the Broken Bottle Lounge as a bouncer and stand-in when the mechanical bull goes on the blink, was more than happy to share with me her can't-miss, five-day, weight-gain plan. "Indulge and bulge," she told me.

MONDAY

BREAKFAST — Pancakes with heavy syrup, a dozen eggs, a loaf of toast and a large watermelon, if in season. If not, substitute a pizza with extra cheese.

LUNCH — A pone of cornbread crumbled into a gallon of buttermilk with a six-pack of tall Pabst as a chaser.

DINNER — A barbecued goat and six Twinkies.

TUESDAY

BREAKFAST — Same as Monday, only add bananas. Enough to feed a family of gorillas for a week.

LUNCH — A school of catfish. Fried. With hush puppies, French fries and enough volume and variety of Girl Scout cookies to buy the local troop an Oldsmobile.

DINNER — A dozen biscuits, smothered in gravy, mashed potatoes with four sticks of butter, a coconut cake and two quarts of Buffalo Rock ginger ale to wash it all down.

WEDNESDAY

BREAKFAST — Grits, served in a large trough, hot with butter and cheese. If you're really hungry, mix in a mess of collards.

LUNCH — Three bowls of chili, a box of Oreos and a long nap.

DINNER — An entire pig, cooked any way you like it. Do not try to put the entire pig in your mouth at once.

THURSDAY

BREAKFAST — A chocolate milkshake, four Hershey bars, three fudgesicles and a half-dozen Reese's Peanut Butter Cups, including the wrappers.

LUNCH — Pig out at McDonald's. If the clown shows up, eat his shoes.

DINNER — Eat a large T-bone steak with all the trimmings. Then drag the bone out in the yard and howl at the moon. Be careful of ticks.

FRIDAY

BREAKFAST — An omelette the size of a Chevy pickup and a large pickle.

LUNCH — A dozen cans of Vienna sausages, a large package of soda crackers and a raw Vidalia onion twice as big as the pickle you had for breakfast.

DINNER — Go to an all-night diner and eat until the sun comes up, or until they run out of food, whichever occurs first. If you get hungry on the way home, stop and buy four dozen Moon Pies and a large jar of mayonnaise.

***

Between the "Single Non-Cookers" diet and Cordie Mae's advice, my body was more confused than I was. Neither of us would have recognized a healthy lifestyle if it had been naked at the beach. In order to save my sanity, I returned to my typewriter and devised "Grizzard's Rationalization Chart of Overeaters, Smokers and Boozers," to be used whenever you slip off the wagon but don't feel like unloading the guilt.

Here's how it works. Food, for instance, will not cause you to gain weight if:

• You eat it standing up.
• You eat it off someone else's plate.
• Your mom cooked it.
• You offer it to the dog first.
• You eat it in the dark.
• You do not chew it.
• You are eating because you're depressed about all the starving people in the world.
• It is smaller than a regulation NBA basketball.
• It's your birthday.
• It's Chester A. Arthur's birthday.

For smokers, there are some equally effective rationalizations. For example, another cigarette won't hurt you if:

• You don't smoke it all the way down to the filter.
• It's not your regular brand.
• You bummed it.

- You throw away the rest of the pack.
- You make a contribution to the American Cancer Society.

Been hitting the bottle a little too hard? One more drink won't hurt you if:
- It's a special occasion, like Happy Hour.
- Something from your past has been eating at you lately, like the death of your dog Skippy when you were four.
- You drink to a worthy cause, like finding a cure for Leon Spinks.
- You use lots of ice.
- The bottle was a gift.
- It was almost empty anyway.
- You make it last longer than the National Hockey League season, which is the only thing that lasts longer than pregnancy.
- You drink it out of a coffee cup.

***

Starting from where I did — that is, uglier than a '47 Packard on blocks — I don't suppose my bad eating, smoking and drinking habits really did all that much harm. They were just a logical extension of me, sort of like clothes.

My clothes. Now, there's another problem. I never could figure out what was in and what was out. When the hippies were wearing sandals, jeans and T-shirts in the late sixties, I was still in my penny loafers, slacks and oxford cloth shirts. By the time my outfit came back into style in the early eighties, I was wearing popsicle-colored leisure suits. In fact, the only people still wearing leisure suits then were me and Slim Whitman.

What did everybody else do with theirs? I admit I haven't been to any bowling league awards banquets or wrestling

151

matches or Moose Club dances lately, but it seems that even that crowd has dumped the leisure suit.

So where are they? They didn't just sprout little polyester legs and walk away. In an attempt to answer this permanent press-ing question, I tried to contact designer Leon "The Needle" Tackeeinksi of Fort Deposit, Alabama, who first introduced the leisure suit to America. Unfortunately, Mr. Tackeeinski could not be located.

"One day," said a man who answered the phone at the Fort Deposit bus station, "he got on the three o'clock northbound and we haven't heard from him since."

When I asked if Mr. Tackeeinski had closed his leisure suit factory before leaving town, the man told me about a mysterious fire the night before his departure which destroyed the entire factory.

"It was a horrible thing," he said. "Half the town was overcome by polyester fumes and couldn't resist the sudden urge to go to Sears-Roebuck and order white shoes and belts."

Perhaps that's the clue I've been looking for to explain what happened to all the leisure suits in this country. Maybe American men, in a burst of fashion consciousness, all went out in their back yards and burned their leisure suits.

"That is highly possible," said a local scientist I contacted about my theory. "As you no doubt have noticed, we have been having strange weather the past few years. One explanation could be that the fumes from all those leisure suits burning rose into the earth's atmosphere, creating what could be called the 'Polyester Zone.' This layer of gases could have a strange effect on our weather. During the hurricane season last year, for instance, I recall that we had one named Delbert that swept in off the Gulf coast and headed straight to the nearest K-Mart."

There is one other possibility about what happened to all the leisure suits. Maybe the Japanese recycled them and are using them to make seat covers for Isuzus. I'm considering using my leisure suits for the same purpose; I'm just not sure how my car will look with orange sherbert-colored seats.

***

The beautiful people of the world, those whose pictures appear on billboards and in television commercials, seldom have to worry about their clothes. If their faces are pretty enough, nobody looks any lower. Or if they have great bodies, nobody cares what they're wearing or even *if* they're wearing. And if they show up dressed in something terribly out of date, people just presume they're being trend-setters.

So why is it that when I show up wearing a blazer with five-inch lapels and Guccis without socks, everybody presumes I'm tacky instead of trendy? Why? Because my face gives it away. No one who looks like Alfred E. Newman can be a trend-setter.

Kathy Sue Loudermilk never had that problem. She was the first real beauty queen I ever knew. She won the coveted Miss Collard Festival Queen title seven years in a row, breaking the record of Cordie Mae Poovey who had won four consecutive titles by threatening the judges.

Kathy Sue turned her victory into a bigtime modeling career and later appeared on a billboard advertisement for Cleghorn Dairies buttermilk. "Cleghorn's Buttermilk — Buy It By the Jugs" is what the copy under Kathy Sue's picture said.

She was justifiably proud of her looks. A reporter for the local newspaper once asked Kathy Sue, "Do you consider yourself a sex symbol?"

She answered him by asking, "Does a duck have lips?"

But many of today's beauty queens can't decide if they're proud of their bodies or embarrassed by them. Half of the contest winners, who've paraded around in bathing suits that wouldn't create suntan lines, say, "I can't stand a man who wants me only for my body. I have a brain, too, and I can use it. I know the capitals of six states and I went to a museum once."

A former Miss Universe from Venezuela said her looks were secondary to her mind. "I want to be an architect and design beautiful buildings," she said. "But buildings with a purpose — for the poor." I'm sure the poor people in Venezuela appreciated that. Give them a few beautiful buildings and maybe they'll quit complaining about being cold and hungry.

Then there are the other beauty queens who are so proud of their endowments that they sometimes forget to keep their clothes on. I recently wrote a treatise on the subject, which I will read at the upcoming Coweta County Moose Club Convention, entitled, "I've Seen England, I've Seen France, I've Seen Miss America Without Her Underpants (With Apologies and Thanks to Vanessa Williams)." I wonder where this new trend will lead?

***

ATLANTIC CITY, NEW JERSEY — DECEMBER, 1999: Twenty-one-year-old Roxanne "Boom Boom" LaTouche, Miss California, was crowned Miss America for 1999 here Saturday evening, becoming the first stripper ever to win the prestigious title.

Miss LaTouche brought both the audience and the judges to their feet with a nude break dance in the talent competition. As pageant emcee Bob Guccione sang the traditional

Miss America theme song, "There She Is, Money in the Bank," Miss LaTouche bumped and grinded down the runway wearing her new crown and, again, to the delight of the all-male audience and male judges, nothing else.

"It just goes to show you," said the beaming Miss LaTouche, "that any girl in this country can become Miss America if she has the correct ideals and values and a new breast implant."

For the last three years, Miss LaTouche has been the star performer at the Yellow Pussy Cat Lounge in Encino, California, where she became famous for her widely heralded ability to strip completely nude while juggling three large cats. Asked if she would return to her position at the lounge, Miss LaTouche announced that she would be attempting instead a career in the movies.

Her agent, Marvin "The Shark" Perronowski, who is also part owner of the Yellow Pussy Cat, said his client is expected to sign a contract with Sin Flick Productions in Hollywood and will star in the full-length porno film titled, "Deep Throat Meets Bert Parks."

Miss LaTouche attended Candy Barr Memorial High School in Encino, where she was captain of the cheerleading squad and became the first cheerleader in the history of the school to have her sweater retired upon graduation.

First runner-up in the pageant was Miss Indiana, who was given temporary parole from the Indiana State Women's Prison in order to compete in the event. She was doing five to ten for armed robbery. Upon learning that she had not won the crown, Miss Indiana pulled a knife on two of the judges but was quickly whisked away by her parole officer.

Second runner-up was Miss Nevada, a stunning Las Vegas showgirl who was named Miss Congeniality by a unanimous vote after a closed-door session with the judges, two of whom — both elderly — were treated and released at a local hospital following the performance.

Third runner-up was Miss New York, daughter of former Miss America Vanessa Williams. Immediately following the contest, Miss New York announced her engagement to Miss Alaska. Former Miss America Williams, incidentally, attended the pageant and told reporters that she plans to enter politics and hopes to be the vice presidential candidate on the Ducks Unlimited ticket in the 2000 presidential election.

Miss LaTouche, meanwhile, begins a national tour next week in which she will make appearances on various talk shows, including the popular NBC "Tonight Show" with host Harry Reems.

"This is one of the best Miss America pageants ever," said Guccione, "and all of our contestants are to be congratulated." Speaking for all contestants, Guccione also said he has more than three thousand nude color photographs of the fifty young women and will run them in the upcoming January edition of his *Penthouse* magazine, which has sponsored the Miss America pageant since 1985.

— 12 —

You've Got to Bend Over
To Pick Grit

FOLLOWING JIMMY AND Billy Carter's rise to national prominence in the late 1970's, the term redneck became very popular with the American public. It was a term of derision in the mouths of some uneducated people, but to those of us born and bred in the South, it was most often used to refer to just good ol' down-to-earth folks. Those of true grit.

Let's say it is your lot in life to have to pick butterbeans. Picking butterbeans is a thankless job that requires long hours of bending over and getting hot and dirty, but somebody has to do it. After a couple of weeks under such conditions, the back of your neck will be redder than the home crowd at a Georgia football game.

Rednecks, or butterbean pickers and others who work the land, have always had trouble with those who see themselves as being more sophisticated just because they happen to live where the bus stops, even if nobody is getting on or off. These people are referred to by rednecks as city slickers. In the mouth of a redneck, city slicker can be a term of derision.

"Hey, redneck," city slickers used to say to a farm boy who ventured into town, "what brings you to civilization?"

"Paw's truck," the redneck inevitably would answer, and the city slickers would have a good bellylaugh. That is, until the redneck plowed on their heads with his fists, which is how rednecks got the reputation of being overly hostile.

Ed Koch, the mayor of New York, is one of those city slickers who doesn't care much for rednecks and the rural way of life. In fact, he once was quoted in a *Playboy* interview as saying that country living was a "joke." My friend Billy Bob Bailey, who was one of the original rednecks and a great American, took offense at Koch's remarks and wrote to tell him so. Billy Bob has given me permission to share his letter, which is now enshrined in cellophane wrapping on the bulletin board at Bogator Green's mechanic and body shop:

> Mayor Ed Koch
> New York City
>
> Dear Mr. Mayor,
>
> My name is Billy Bob Bailey and I live in Fort Deposit, Alabama, which is so far back in the country that the sun goes down somewhere between here and Montgomery, the state capital.
>
> I was over to the store the other evening and they had the television on and I heard what you said about living out in the country. You said

driving around in a pickup truck and driving twenty miles to buy a Sears-Roebuck suit was a waste of time. You said living in the country was a "joke." What kind of fumes have you been inhaling, your honor?

I drive a pickup truck, and one advantage to living out here in the country is the only time I ever get stuck in traffic is when there's a funeral and the hearse breaks down. Those of us in line have to wait until Junior (he's the funeral director's son) goes back to the plant and gets the jumper cables. You got that wrong about Sears-Roebuck suits, too. I don't wear no suits, period. No need to. They don't care what you wear to the Moose Club, long as you ain't barefooted.

They started requiring shoes because of Hoot Dingler, who used to come in regularly to drink beer and shoot pool and was always barefooted. Hoot didn't even own any shoes. Didn't believe in 'em. "Might slow me down if I needed to get somewhere in a hurry," Hoot explained. Problem was that Hoot's a pig farmer and he's always walking around where the pigs live. We might be country, but we don't like to drink beer, shoot pool and smell hog at the same time, so they changed the rule about coming in barefooted. Hoot started drinking with the Elks after that.

They showed a picture of you on television, Mr. Mayor, and you look right slack-eyed and loop-legged to me. Been a little bilious and goofy-headed lately? Sometime when folks don't feel good, they say things they don't mean. I hope you didn't mean what you said about living in the

159

country being a joke, 'cause my dog Rooster heard about it, too (he reads the Montgomery newspaper), and Rooster don't like nobody from New York City throwing off on the way we live. "I wouldn't shoot a rat trying to crawl out of New York City," is what Rooster always says.

If I were you, Mr. Mayor, I wouldn't come around Fort Deposit or Rooster for awhile, because I'm afraid that dog would take a plug out of your leg and I couldn't stop him with a stick.

Rooster and me ain't never been to New York City, but it ain't exactly Hog Heaven either, is what we hear. Vonda Kay Potts from right here in Fort Deposit was state dairy queen one year and won a trip to New York City. She said she liked it fine except that when you went outside, the streets and air were so dirty that the whole place smelled like Hoot Dingler's feet.

We hear that you want to further your political career after you're through being mayor. Maybe be governor or president or something. But I wouldn't count on a lot of support from the rural parts of the nation, Mr. Mayor. It's like Rooster always says: Country people all have one thing in common. They know a rat trying to crawl out of New York City when they see one.

Thanks, all,
Billy Bob Bailey

***

Billy Bob's right when he says that life in the country can be awfully good. I was reminded of that fact recently when I ran into an old friend I hadn't seen since college. He now owns a small drugstore in a small South Georgia town. He has the same wife he started out with and two babies and a dog, a cat and a number of hogs.

"My hog farm is my hobby," he says. "When I'm out there with them, I can really relax."

Maybe Mayor Koch and everyone else who struggles to survive in our cities should take note. Give everybody a small hog farm and maybe there would be less crime and fewer heart attacks.

My old friend also is a member of the city council in his town. "I get $75 a month, and it's rare I get cussed out more than twice a week." He is involved in local charities and organizes an annual tennis tournament which raises money for the county retardation center. My friend donates the hogs for the barbecue which is held in conjunction with the tournament, and the ladies in town bake pies and cookies and make potato salad and cole slaw, and somebody slices a mile of tomatoes. The only thing wrong with any of this lifestyle, my friend says, is the gnats. "We call 'em the South Georgia Air Force."

Comparing my life in the city with his in the country makes me stop and think. He lives the solid rural life and helps sick folks and tries to make his community a better place to live. And in between all that, he raises hogs and children and breaks his butt trying to help those who have trouble helping themselves. Me, I rattle around with a couple million hurrying souls and we fight traffic and each other. Sometimes all I get from the effort is the blues.

They might not believe it on the flat, piney plains of South Georgia, but there are worse things in life than gnats.

***

Of course, life in rural America can be filled with excitement, too. There are more characters in most small towns than gnats in South Georgia. Just the other day a friend was telling me a story about a fellow named Paul in his hometown.

"Paul was having some trouble with the IRS, something about an unauthorized deduction. So when these two IRS men wanted to meet with him, he told them to come down to where he lives — in a trailer way back in the woods with the snakes and armadillos and albino possums — to have lunch.

"Paul, you know, eats about a quart of mayonnaise every day, so he reached into his mayonnaise jar, pulled out a handful, and started spreading it on bread. That's all he wanted on his sandwich, but he put a slice or two of meat on those other fellows'. He sat down at the table, pulled out his gun from one pocket and his brass knuckles from another and laid them on the table. Then he asked the two IRS men to join him in prayer.

"'Lord,' he started, 'please keep these two fellows safe while they're here with me, because you know how much I want to shoot 'em. But, Lord, don't let me do that, much as I want to....' When Paul looked up from praying, the two IRS men were gone. He ain't heard a word from them since."

***

Rural Americans, especially those in the South, have long been misunderstood by other segments of the population. Some folks think just because a fellow has a gun rack in the back window of his pickup that he's on his way to shoot a bunch of liberals. They think grits grow on trees and poke salad is a weed. And possibly their biggest misconception of all is that the pink plastic flamingos positioned in many front yards are "tacky."

Nothing could be further from the truth. Tasteful, well-bred individuals normally paint the trunks of the trees in their yards white; line their driveways with old tires, also painted white; plant flowers between the tires; and place at least three pink flamingos strategically about the lawn.

Common riffraff, meanwhile, decorate their yards by taking the tires off a '52 Studebaker and putting the automobile on cement blocks beside the house.

I remember the day my family moved into a new home. How I swelled with pride when my parents allowed me to stick the legs of our new plastic pink flamingos in our front yard.

"Does this mean we are a tasteful, well-bred family and no longer common riffraff?" I asked.

"It does, indeed, son," answered my mother.

How could anyone, even an unenlightened yankee person, refer to plastic pink flamingos as "tacky"? They lend a tropical flair to any yard. They are graceful in their posture, and their pink color blends most pleasingly with the green hue of the grass, just as a red shirt accentuates a black polyester suit.

My boyhood friend and idol, Weyman C. Wannamaker, Jr., a great American, had a dozen plastic pink flamingos in his yard. Weyman's mother was president of the local garden club, and her yard was the annual winner of the "House Beautiful" award in our community.

Mrs. Wannamaker, being a woman of exceeding taste and breeding, complemented her flamingos with a ceramic hen being followed by her baby chicks, and various other lawn statuary including ducks and deer and one marvelous piece in the form of a fat Sumo wrestler, which she got for free when she purchased four chenille bedspreads.

Mrs. Wannamaker's yard was also quite impressive at Christmas. Her annual decoration included Santa's sleigh being pulled by — you guessed it — eight pink flamingos.

When asked about his mother's Christmas decorations, Weyman said, "My mother is a very sick person."

I would like to add in closing that I have just purchased a new home and have ordered two pair of pink flamingos from the Sears catalog. I haven't decided for sure, but I think I'm going to put them next to the little birdhouse that says, "See Rock City" on the roof.

My neighbors will be pink with envy.

***

So country ain't so bad after all. And if you don't believe it, try calling Ed Koch the next time you have a craving for a big pot of butterbeans.

— 13 —

The Bigger They Are, The More They Weigh

NOT EVERYBODY GETS out of life what they put into it. Some folks work hard all their days and never free themselves from the bog of poverty. Others just bounce through life like a pinball, taking the easiest path but lighting up things and racking up points all the way. Yet from one end of the tax scale to the other, from Who's Who to the welfare rolls, real character looks the same.

A GENTLE BEAR OF A MAN

I spent an afternoon drinking with Paul "Bear" Bryant once. I had been to Athens, Georgia, with him for an autographing session for the book he wrote with John Underwood of *Sports Illustrated*. When we returned to the Atlanta airport, there were still a couple of hours before his flight to Tuscaloosa, Alabama.

"Let's get a drink," he said.

The weather was awful. Rain. High winds. Lightning and thunder. Bad flying weather. Good drinking weather. He took me into the Eastern Ionosphere Lounge, where he ordered double Black Jack and Coke. Two at a time.

I probably got the best interview of my life that afternoon, but I don't remember much of it. However, I do remember walking him back to the departure gate two hours later. At the gate, the Bear ran into a doctor from Tuscaloosa who was booked on the same flight. The doctor was also an amateur pilot.

"Coach," said the doctor, "I don't like this weather."

"You a drinking man, son?" Bryant asked him.

"Yes, sir," said the doctor.

"Well, good. Let's get us a couple of motel rooms and have a drink and fly home tomorrow."

There were fifty or sixty would-be passengers awaiting the same flight to Tuscaloosa. When they saw Bear Bryant turning in his ticket, all but a handful did the same thing.

"If Bear Bryant is afraid to fly in this weather," one man said, "I sure as hell ain't about to."

That was the last time I was with the Bear. On January 26, 1983, he died of a heart attack. As soon as I heard the news, I knew I had to get in touch with a friend of mine.

She had met Bear Bryant through her profession, public relations, several years earlier, but their relationship had grown far beyond that. I'm not talking hanky-panky here; grandfather and granddaughter comes closest to describing it.

They were an unlikely pair. He, the gruff, growling old coot of a football coach. She, a bright, young, attractive woman with both a husband and a career and a degree from the University of Texas, of all places.

He would call her even in the middle of football season and they would talk, and he would do her any favor. Once a friend of hers, a newspaper columnist, was having heart surgery. She called the Bear and had him send the fellow a scowling picture with the autograph, "I hope you get well soon. Bear Bryant." The picture still hangs in my home.

I called her the minute I heard that he had died. I didn't want her to get it on the radio. She cried.

"I loved him," she said, "and he loved my baby."

My friend had had a baby a few years earlier. Had it been a boy, she would have named him for the Bear, David Bryant. But it was a girl, and so she named her Marissa.

"I had no problems with naming my son David Bryant, but I wasn't about to name a little girl Beara," said my friend.

Of course, a busy, big-time college football coach like Bear Bryant didn't give it a second thought that somebody else's little girl wasn't named for him. He still sent her gifts. Gifts like a child's Alabama cheerleader uniform, and then an adult-size uniform for use later. He sent her footballs, dolls and probably a dozen or so letters that her mama read to her.

It's funny, though. When he sent his packages and letters, he always addressed them not to Marissa but "To Paula."

LAUGHTER IN THE SKY

Great big ol' Jerry Clower was signing an autograph when I spotted him in a busy airport. Great entertainers need neither stage nor special occasion as opportunity to perform. An airport or an airplane, for instance, is just as good as any.

For the uninformed, Jerry Clower of Yazoo, Mississippi, used to go around telling funny stories and selling fertilizer. Then somebody from Nashville discovered him and signed him to a recording contract. Now all Jerry does is go around telling funny stories, although some insist that he's still spreading verbal fertilizer.

On the plane, Jerry took a seat in front of me, turned around and began to spout forth his philosophy on any number of subjects in a voice loud enough to be heard throughout the plane. With Jerry Clower around, E.F. Hutton would never get a word in edgewise.

I asked him about a mutual friend, a writer.

"We agree on lots of things," he said of the fellow, "but we're a lot different, too. Like, I've been married to the same woman (Homerline) for thirty-seven years. He's been livin' with one about two years and says he don't know if they're going to get married or not because he ain't through trying her out yet."

I mentioned something about college football and his eyes lit up. Jerry used to play a little offensive line at Mississippi State.

"What I like most about college football," he said, "are the rivalries. I was down at the University of Texas the other day. They don't like Texas A&M one bit, you know. Fellow down at Texas told me the Texas A&M men are so lazy that they marry pregnant women."

The passengers, all of them, were his by now, so he kept rolling.

"These network news fellows always amaze me. Big reservoir down in Mississippi has been flooding for years, but up until last year it was just the poor blacks and poor whites who were being flooded out. Then some of them $200,000 houses started gettin' a little mud inside 'em, and it all of a sudden is a big story.

"This network news fellow went down there to one of them big houses and asked this proper woman what she thought caused the flood. She said it was the bass fishermen. She said they hadn't lowered the reservoir enough just so them bass fishermen could still catch fish. Then he interviewed this real intelligent man. He blamed the whole thing on the Corps of Engineers, said they hadn't planned the watershed right.

"Course, them network fellows try not to interview no good ol' boys when they come to Mississippi, 'cause they think they don't know nothing. But one of 'em slipped up and interviewed this ol' boy he figured was highfaluting 'cause he happened to be wearing a coat and tie. He asked him what he thought caused the flood. 'Sixteen inches of rain caused it, and if we get that much rain next year, we'll have another flood.' "

Jerry also told his boots story. He was on a Hollywood talk show one time and a lady producer noticed his boots.

"She jumped up out of her chair like a wasp had done stung her," he said, "and she commenced to hollering about my boots. She said, 'What kind of boots are those, Mr. Clower?' And I said, 'These here are lizard boots.'

"She said, 'I can't believe you would wear such boots. To think that somebody killed an innocent little animal just so you could wear those boots.' I said, 'No, ma'am. This particular lizard was run over by a Greyhound bus. I even stood out there in the road and helped fight the buzzards off him.' "

There was a pause and then Jerry Clower added, "You know, I sometimes get the feeling some people are educated far beyond their intelligence."

And anyone who has spent much time with Jerry Clower

has been blessed far beyond his due.

HE'S THE ONE IN OVERALLS

They buried Junior Samples in his favorite pair of overalls on a cold Georgia day, dark and damp, in November 1983. Junior's bronze, flower-laden casket was closed during the services, but a man standing outside the church confirmed that Junior's family wasn't about to send him across the river wearing anything else.

"All Junior ever wore was overalls, anyway," said the man.

"One thing's for sure," said another, "he's a lot more comfortable than he would have been in a pair of britches."

Junior Samples, Forsyth County's claim to fame, died of a heart attack at age fifty-six. Slow talking, slow moving Junior turned a fish story somebody recorded back in the sixties into a career as a bungling bumpkin on television's "Hee Haw."

Junior's funeral was inside the little white-frame Roanoke Baptist Church out on the Buford Dam Road. An Atlanta television cameraman remarked what a pretty picture the little church made, perched atop a hill, its steeple and cross reaching toward the gray sky.

"These folks up here had a lot of respect for Junior," said a local reporter. "What they liked about him, he didn't change after he got on TV. He still got out amongst folks. He was one of them right until the end."

It was generally agreed that Junior's was one of the biggest funerals in the county's history. Early arrivals got seats inside the church, but by the time the Jenkins Family, local gospel singers, opened the services with "One Day at a Time, Sweet Jesus" and "Just a Rose," there were more gathered on the porch of the church and in the muddy driveway than were inside.

A man from the funeral home told me about Junior's flowers.

"We loaded up a truck plumb full," he said, "and we still got just as many back at the funeral home."

I asked if he had known Junior personally.

"Knowed him all my life," he answered proudly. "People thought he was trying to be funny on television, but he was just being Junior."

Another group of Junior's friends gathered under a barren tree outside the church. The blue hearse pulled up first. Junior's tearful family followed. Next came a Tennessee sheriff's car with some of "Hee Haw"'s other stars.

"There's LuLu," said one of the men. "She looks as fat in person as she does on television, don't she?" She did.

Nobody knew her real name, but the toothless woman who's always beating her husband over the head on the program came, too.

"I thought they made her up to look that ugly," said another onlooker. "Lord, she's just natural ugly."

A tall, blonde woman they identified as Misty Roe, one of the "Hee Haw" girls, got the most attention. She wore high heels and a black miniskirt, and her hair had been teased into a frazzled, frenzied mane.

"Looks like she'd knowed not to have dressed thataway," somebody said.

The boys outside said Junior hadn't been drinking as much the last few months since he had been so sick. The preacher told mourners inside the church that Junior hadn't been doing as much fishing lately, either.

"He knew the final hour was upon him," the preacher said. "And he spent his last days praying. I can tell you

Junior Samples was saved. His name was recorded on the Lamb's Roll of Life."

The Jenkins Family ended the service with "Shall We Gather at the River," and everybody went home, content that Junior was with the angels.

In case you don't watch much television, Lord, he's the one in overalls.

A STORY OF COURAGE AND DIGNITY

She said she remembered the first time she ever saw him. "I was in a seventh-grade music class in my hometown of Provo, Utah," she began. "The teacher introduced us to a new boy who had just moved into town from New York. He was wearing knickers. He had on a pullover sweater and a little cap. He wore them every day. I found out later he was so poor that's all his mother could afford."

They became friends. They moved on to high school together, and they attended dances together.

"He told me there were two reasons he took me to dances," she recalled. "He said he liked me, of course, but I also had paid for my activities card, so he didn't have to pay a nickel to get me in."

Una Clark is a bright, pert lady with an easy smile. She lives in Seattle, Washington. Does her name sound familiar? That's right, Mrs. Barney Clark, widow of the first human recipient of an artificial heart. Dr. Barney Clark, the little boy in knickers, grew up to be a dentist. He developed heart problems, and when there was no alternative, he agreed to try the artificial heart. It kept him alive 112 days.

"We did hope there would be personal gain if we agreed to the artificial heart," said Mrs. Clark, "but Barney also felt this was something he could do for his fellow man. Somebody had to be first."

I wanted to know more about Una and Barney Clark's life together. After Dr. Clark died, his doctor said one of the reasons he was able to live as long as he did was because of the strong support he had from his family, because he had a wife who loved him dearly. I wanted to know how such a relationship came about.

"Barney never had much confidence," Mrs. Clark said. "He never told me how he felt about me. His father had died when he was very young, and he had been so insecure, so poor. I think that's what caused his lack of confidence. Maybe if he had said he cared about me, something would have happened when we were younger, but I never had any idea he wanted anything serious between us. I married his best friend."

That was just before the outbreak of World War II. Una Clark's husband was a flier. He died in action.

"Barney called me when he heard what had happened," she said. "It wasn't long after that when we found out we loved each other."

Dr. Barney Clark was a bombardier during the war. It was his service record, said his wife, that gave him the confidence he had never had before. He went to dental school after the war and established a successful practice.

"Everything he did, he went after it hard," said Una Clark. "If there was anything about him I could criticize, it would be that he was selfish with his time. He was a workaholic. If I could have changed him, I would have made him spend more time with me."

The man showed awesome courage in agreeing to become the first artificial heart recipient. His last days were spent in the discomfort of tubes and tests. But as his wife said, somebody had to be first. As one who has benefited directly from heart research, Una and Barney Clark are heroes to me.

One more thing I had to ask. "Do you miss him?"

"Yes," she answered softly. "I miss him very much."

We all do.

FORGIVE HIM AND TOAST HIS MEMORY

Marvin Griffin was governor of the State of Georgia from 1955-59. When he died in 1982, most of his eulogies included an apology for the fact that he once stood tall for segregation.

Running for political office has a lot in common with show business. You give the people what they want. When Marvin Griffin ran for governor, what the people of Georgia wanted — at least those who could vote — was a segregationist. If you felt differently in those days, about the only thing you could run for was the state line.

I'm not launching a defense of Marvin Griffin's politics; I'm just pointing out that he wasn't singing a solo.

As a person, I liked him very much. I first met him a dozen years ago in a bar. I introduced myself and told him my grandfather had been one of his most ardent admirers.

"What is yo' granddaddy's name, son?" he asked me.

I told him.

"Yes, indeed," said the former governor. "A fine man. I know him well. And how is his health?"

"Been dead ten years," I answered.

"Sorry to hear that, son," said Uncle Marvin. "Let's toast his memory."

Some are born to politick, and I've never drunk with a better practitioner of the art. He had a million great lines, and he growled them in a classic Southernese. He was a big man, robust and full of life. When he talked, he played with each word, milking it for all it was worth.

He was asked once, after his term as governor was over, if he had any advice for young politicians. "Tell 'em to remember just two things," he said. "Keep yo' mouth shut and yo' bowels open."

The last time I saw him was at a banquet before a big Georgia football game. He was the opening speaker and forgot at least the first part of his advice to young politicians. The thousands assembled nearly missed the kickoff of the football game, but I loved every minute of it. There'll be other games, but only one Marvin Griffin.

"Man came up to me one time when I was campaigning in Fayette County," he reminisced, "and said, 'Governor, let's me and you go have a little drink.' I said, 'My friend, soon as I see to it that everybody in Fayette County knows my name, I'll go drink a mule's earful with you.' "

Forgive him his opportunistic bellowings for segregation. Forgive him the improprieties of his administration. He added color to our lives and made us some memories, he did. A mule's earful.

— 14 —

Please Adjust
Your Set

E VERY TIME I HEAR about the modern communications explosion, I keep hoping that somebody has
finally blown up most of the television and radio stations
and about half of the newspapers in this country.

We are, in fact, besieged with words, spoken and written. There probably are more satellite dishes in rural America today than there are tractors. In the words of a sixties
rock hit, "Signs, signs, everywhere signs, funking up the
scenery, breaking my mind. Do this. Don't do that. Can't
you read the signs?"

Being able to decipher all these communications, to cull
the good from the bad, the useful from the useless, the
helpful from the harmful, is one of the traits of those who
possess true grit. The rest of us merely dog paddle through
this alphabet soup. Me, I've progressed to the back stroke.

Just driving to work and reading the signs along the way

can overload your circuits. "Watch for Falling Rocks," says a frequent one. But how, I ask myself, can I watch for falling rocks and at the same time keep from running my car off the accompanying cliff?

"Low Flying Aircraft" is another of my favorite highway signs. Why are they telling me that? It's not flying that low, is it? And what am I supposed to do if I see a low-flying aircraft? Blow my horn and wave? My policy regarding low-flying aircraft is I won't bother them if they won't bother me.

There are signs on many entrances to interstate highways which read, "Take Gap, Give Gap." In public? Sounds like something that ought to wait until you get to a motel room.

I was in a radio station in Austin, Texas, recently. In the vending and coffee area was a sign that read, "Your mother doesn't work here, so clean up after yourself."

Here are some other favorites I've encountered along the way:

• In a Hilton Head, South Carolina, health food store: "Anyone having the audacity to smoke in here will be flogged unmercifully with an organic banana."

• Above a pool table in a roadhouse in Oklahoma: "No gambling. Anybody caught gambling will be prosuted." It's bad enough when they prosute in a doctor's office, much less in a pool hall.

• Handwritten on the front window of a South Alabama service station: "This here is a service station. It ain't no bank. Don't come in here and ask me to cash no checks. And that includes kinfolks."

• In front of a large Baptist church in Atlanta: "Caution: Blind People Crossing."

• In front of a used car lot in Spartanburg, South Carolina, which had closed for the night: "This lot is guarded by armed security three nights a week. Guess which three."

Of course, the most common signs of all are not printed but scrawled — graffiti. And New York, where everyone is handed a paint brush as they cross the East River, is the graffiti capital of the world. Writing on the sides of subway cars is as much a tradition in New York as a $14.95 breakfast in a hotel restaurant.

What I've never understood is how somebody can run alongside a speeding subway train with a can of spray paint and still be able to write "BJ Is One Bad Hombre" legibly. The trains don't stop long enough in the stations to get a shot at them standing still, so I assume BJ is also one fast hombre.

If it weren't for the damage done to public and private property, I would be in favor of graffiti. Not everyone in America can write a column for a newspaper or be a television or radio commentator. There are even a couple of people left in the country who have never spoken to a Rotary Club. For those Americans, graffiti can be an invaluable source of expression. Let me give you an example:

There is a freeway overpass near Atlanta's Hartsfield Airport, by some counts the world's busiest. A message has been painted on it. In black paint and in a scraggly handwriting, it says, "Betty. You Are Missed."

Betty. You are missed. I can't stop my imagination when it comes to that message. The guy is almost dying. He's tried everything. He's called all her friends. Her mother. She didn't even leave a note. Just up and went east. He came home from work — he drives a cab nights — and she was gone. Took her clothes, the albums, the pictures of the bullfighter, and left him with an empty bed and that awful pain that crawls down in your belly and does a dance that won't let you eat, sleep or put two sane thoughts back to back.

Regrets. First he goes through all his regrets. He never took her out. Maybe twice a month they would go get a pizza. Even then she would want anchovies, and he hated anchovies, so they wouldn't order them, and she would get that disappointed look on her face and pooch out her lips. God, she was cute when she pooched out her lips that way. If he could just find her, he'd buy her a truckload of anchovies.

He forgot her last birthday. He should have been more tender. He should have kissed her on her nose occasionally and said mushy things to her. He'd wanted to, but it's tough for some men to do things like that, and he thought she knew that he felt it but just didn't know how to get it out.

He goes for a few beers one night. Alone. Somebody punches B-6 on the jukebox. Willie Nelson. "You Were Always on My Mind." He drinks half a case, remembers the can of spray paint in his cab, drives to the overpass and, with a shaking hand, does the last desperate thing he knows to do. "Betty. You Are Missed."

Maybe one day, I always think, she will see the message and recognize his handwriting and come back home and be up to her ears in anchovies and kisses on the nose. Or maybe she won't. But I have to believe that man felt a little better that night after he sprayed his message on the freeway overpass. As long as the message is there, as long as some yo-yo from the highway department doesn't come along and remove it, he has hope, some slight shade of hope.

I haven't yet succumbed to writing my messages on freeway overpasses, but I've cried out in a similar way. I have a lingering case of Black Cord Fever. This ailment is easily diagnosed. All you have to do is check your monthly long-distance telephone bill. Is the total $11.16? Then relax, you don't have it. Is it $133.28? Does it include calls to places like Anchorage and Hershey? If so, you've got it bad.

Black Cord Fever is a condition that causes people to get an irresistable urge to make long distance calls in the middle of the night. Let's say it's two o'clock in the morning, you've had a couple of toots and start missing your old girl friend Gloria, who stole the mattress from your apartment and moved to Toledo.

"That you Gloria?" you ask when the ringing finally stops.

"Izme," she answers.

"Are you asleep?" you ask. Another symptom of BCF is that you ask stupid questions. Of course, she's asleep. Everyone in Toledo is asleep at two in the morning.

Turns out Gloria is now living with Freddy, who has the phone by this time, and he threatens to reach out and touch your head with a large stick if he ever gets the chance.

Realizing the love of your life and that creep Freddy are probably sleeping on the very mattress she stole from your apartment, you become very sad and call your ex-wife in Omaha. The only thing she didn't take when she left was the mattress that Gloria got. A man suffering from BCF can run up a huge long-distance bill in one night of tracking down ex-girlfriends, ex-wives and ex-mattresses.

I'm convinced that the telephone companies are directly responsible for BCF in this country. Those conductors of words are the ones who're always trying to embarrass us into calling somebody. That's really your mother they picture in their commercials, looking sad that she hasn't heard from her darling in months. "He's forgotten all about me.

181

He doesn't love me anymore. I know because he never calls," is what your mother says in those commercials.

So you give in and call. Turns out your mother is at the wrestling match and you get Uncle Willie, who just had his gallbladder removed. And it costs you twenty-six bucks to hear him describe his operation. In detail. You'd just as soon talk to that creep Freddy.

Next time Black Cord Fever strikes, I may just reach for a can of spray paint. Another couple of words won't matter at this point.

Another way phones contribute to media pollution is telephone solicitation. I answer and a woman's voice asks, "Are you the man of the house?" I know I don't sound like Broderick Crawford, but I sure don't sound like Aunt Sally come to visit from Shreveport, either.

Usually they're selling portraits. If you can answer a question — "Who was the only American president to resign from office? His initials are R.N." — you win a free family portrait worth $17.95. The idea, of course, is to sucker you into taking the entire family down to the studio for one free portrait, but by the time they've finished taking individual shots of all the young'uns, they're into you for big bucks.

The other day, however, I got a different scam. A woman who sounded about fifteen years old asked, "As you prepared to invest $29.95 for a selection of coupons worth thousands of dollars if you went out and bought each item for yourself?"

Before I could answer, she was off and running.

"I'm certain you are, so allow me to describe what you will be receiving by purchasing these valuable coupons from Earl's Midnight Merchandising Company. First, you will get a free lube job, wheel balancing, front end alignment, wash and wax, two tanks of gas, an oil change including a new filter, one set of spark plugs and three quarts of transmission fluid.

"You also will receive a free membership to the Reverend Leon Goforth's Spiritual Health Spa, including one free consultation with Reverend Goforth hisself, who will tell you how you can find salvation through deep knee-bends. This offer also includes free Putt-Putt golf, four trips down Willie's Wild 'n' Wet Water Slide, a case of ping-pong balls and a year's free bowling at Lucky's Pin-o-Matic Lanes, including shoe rental.

"Don't think this is all you will receive from this once-in-a-lifetime opportunity, however, 'cause there's much, much more. You will also get one honey-baked ham, a case of Diet Pepsi Free, three packages of luncheon meat, a free subscription to People Magazine and nine baby chicks, guaranteed live on arrival. Then you'll get a night's free stay at Purdy's Bide-a-Wee Motel in the fabulous Rock City resort area, a pet goat, a nine-by-twelve color photograph, suitable for framing, of the Wilburn brothers and volumes A through M of the Encyclopedia Britannica."

The girl had not breathed in five minutes, but I was afraid to stop her.

"And that's not all. You will be receiving a man's and a woman's Timex watch, a Tennessee Ernie Ford album collection of inspirational hymns, two bamboo steamers, a pocket fisherman, a tea strainer and three live Maine lobsters.

"For one payment and one payment only of $29.95, you will be entitled to all that and more, including a free estimate from the Mug-a-Bug man, a Hertz once-a-month flea and tick collar for your dog or cat, a year's supply of Preparation H, a package of Velveeta cheese, a road map of Idaho, the complete works of Zane Grey, a dozen personalized No. 2 lead pencils, seven pairs of ladies' underpants with each day of the week printed on the backs and a Shetland pony named Arnold.

"Now, will someone from your family be at home for the next hour so that one of our sales representatives can drop by and allow you to take advantage of this fabulous offer?"

I asked her if she would mind reading the list to me one more time, that I thought I had missed a couple of important things. When she got to the part about transmission fluid, I softly depressed the button and hung up.

***

Television obviously is the biggest culprit when it comes to communications pollution, and nowhere is the pollution more evident than in TV weather reports. You can actually see it. Those high-priced meteorologists (a week before, they were slapping hoods in used car commercials) don't call it pollution, of course; they refer to it as "ground clutter."

"Looking on the hundred mile scan of our Super-Duper Weather Scooper, you'll see that it's completely clear. All those patches of color that look like torrential rain are really just ground clutter that the radar is picking up."

I'm still not sure what "ground clutter" is. Will it stick to the soles of my shoes? Will it cause ring worm? If there's nothing on the radar, why do they spend so much time showing it anyway?

Ludlow Porch, who included a weather report in his popular radio talk show, had a better way of dealing with the weather. He'd send his dog outside. "If Rover came back wet, I knew right away that it was raining. If he came back with ice on him, I knew it was cold. That's really all anybody needs to know about the weather. The rest is just pollution."

The best weatherperson I ever knew was my grandmother, Mama Willie. She watched the weather like a hawk.

"Looks like it's about to come up a cloud," she would say. "Come up a cloud" is Deep South for, "It's about to rain."

Mama Willie always knew when it was about to rain because the corns on her little toe would ache. When the corns on her big toe ached, it meant fair to partly cloudy. Mama Willie also had a unique way of forecasting cold.

"Going to turn cold soon," she would say.

"How can you tell?" I would ask.

"Saw a hog frowning today," she would answer. "He knows what's coming."

I've never seen a hog frown or smile, but by the time they get to the stage I like them — sausage, bacon and barbecue — facial expressions are pretty much a thing of the past. Then again, maybe they smile only in the summer; if that's so, I also never would have seen one, because nobody in his right mind goes near a hog dwelling when it's hot.

Late one spring we had a frost which Mama Willie failed to predict. "It's them satellites," she said. "Fouls up the weather. Shame none of them astronauts don't have any chickens to worry about. Maybe then they'd think about staying on the ground."

Then again, maybe chickens are responsible for ground clutter.

***

Television soap operas are another form of television pollution. Does that stuff really go on in the suburbs? And if so, what kinds of vitamins are those guys taking?

I haven't spent much time watching them, but it seems to me that all the soaps I've seen follow the same formula. So I figured if other folks are getting rich from packaging the same sleaze over and over, I might as well give it a try myself. Thus, Grizzard Entertainment proudly presents "General Popsicle" — love, lust and other steamy stuff you used to have to go to the movies to see, set in a Baskin-Robbins ice cream parlor in a shopping center on the outskirts of Bismarck, North Dakota.

The cast:

• NORENE — Sexy eighteen-year-old vaporhead who works the counter during the early shift. Still has trouble telling the difference between chocolate and vanilla. "I know one is dark and one isn't," she says, which at least indicates a step in the right direction. Wears tight-fitting uniforms and brings in customers from miles around who have no interest in ice cream but enjoy watching Norene shake her pistachio.

• DORENE — Sexy eighteen-year-old vaporhead who works the counter during the late shift. Gets confused when a customer asks for more than one scoop of any flavor. The mop has a higher IQ. Also wears tight-fitting uniforms and is so well endowed that she once reached deep into a bucket of almond toffee and was stuck there for nearly an hour until the Roto-Rooter man could be summoned to free her. There was no charge for his services.

• ARNOLD — Assistant manager who flunked out of the Bismarck School of Bartending. Twenty-ish, handsome, smiles out of the corner of his mouth and steals out of the cash register to support his Clearasil addiction.

• MR. PALMER — The manager. Forty-ish, balding, former wrestler and veterinarian. Friendly and fatherlike to his employees, especially Norene and Dorene. Likes Arnold, too, but is suspicious of him. "I wouldn't trust him as far as I could throw the mop," says Mr. Palmer.

• THE MOP — Has more acting ability than anyone else in the cast.

The show opens as Norene and Dorene vie for Arnold's attention. They get into a huge, hair-pulling, name-calling fight behind the counter over near the chocolate mint, and Mr. Palmer has to break it up. During the confusion of the fight, the refrigeration system is accidentally shut off and six thousand gallons of ice cream melt and begin to run all over the floor and out into the parking lot of the shopping center.

As the melting ice cream shorts out the center's lighting system, Arnold goes from store to store cleaning out the cash registers and then splits for Fargo in Mr. Palmer's black 1958 Buick.

Norene and Dorene, their uniforms torn in revealing fashion during the fight, both tell Mr. Palmer they are pregnant and that Arnold is the father of their babies. Mr. Palmer marries both Norene and Dorene because that's the only honorable thing to do, and the Roto-Rooter man reappears to demand payment for freeing Dorene from the almond toffee.

Millions of dollars in lawsuits result from the ice cream meltdown, and Mr. Palmer is now completely broke. He decides to commit suicide by sticking his head in a bucket of chocolate syrup. Before he can do so, however, Arnold, who has used the money he stole from the shopping center to stage a successful campaign and become governor of North Dakota, returns to the scene and pays off all of Mr. Palmer's debts.

Norene and Dorene find out they weren't really pregnant after all, and they run away with the Roto-Rooter man. The mop falls off the wall in disgust.

Next on "General Popsicle": Mr. Palmer hires a new coun-

187

ter girl. Or is she? Guest appearance by Renee Richards.

***

Actually the soap operas are no more offensive than the television commercials which run with them. Take those feminine hygiene products, for example. One manufacturer touts the fact that its products are disposable. Now, I ask you: Who would want to keep such a thing?

Deodorant commercials are the same way. "Oh, Marge," says one Junior Leaguer to another, "how do you manage to stay so dry?" I'll tell you how Marge manages to stay so dry. She lies around in bed all day eating bon-bons and not hitting a lick at a snake, that's how.

I saw a commercial the other day for medicine to remove canker sores. What on earth are canker sores and where do they come from? Do you get them on your canker, and if so, where is mine?

Recently attorneys have gotten into the act. They show pictures of rear-end collisions where everybody ends up with whiplash. Then they follow with a cute little jingle, like,

Wilson, Jones, Morris and Pate, The ones to call when you lit-ah-gate.

May they get sores on their cankers, and may their wives dispose of their feminine hygiene products by storing them in their husbands' golf bags.

And then there's the commercial for burial plots which begins, "We started not to make this commercial...." So why did you, casket face? It was that commercial which convinced me to give my body to science when I die. I want them to figure out how a man in my condition could live so long.

***

But to paraphrase an old adage, there's some good in the

188

worst of everything, even television. Amid all that harmless (or is it mindless?) clutter, there occasionally is a program that can make you think. And squirm.

The best squirmmaker of them all, I suspect, is "60 Minutes." Sunday after Sunday, Mike Wallace always gets his man.

"And so, Mr. Ferndorf, you say you know nothing whatsoever about the falsified expense reports," Mike Wallace says, and his victim, that lying cheat Ferndorf, thinks he's about to get off the hook.

"I know nothing about it, Mike," says Ferndorf, who is sadly mistaken.

"Then what about these?" asks Wallace, suddenly producing from some unknown place the falsified expense reports. And guess whose signature is all over them.

Ferndorf, dead duck, begins to squirm.

"We're waiting, Mr. Ferndorf," says Wallace, twisting the knife.

"Well...I, huh," explains Ferndorf, who by now is perspiring and turning blue while all of America watches.

"Look at this, Martha," says the average "60 Minutes" viewer in Des Moines. "Ol' Mike just got another one!"

As a squirmmaker, Perry Mason was small time compared to Mike Wallace.

I have this recurring dream, part of the Mike Wallace Syndrome, where "60 Minutes" gets in touch with me and says they would like to get some footage for a possible future profile. This is my big break, I think, and soon all the cameras are there and I'm sitting across from Mike Wallace and we're having a lovely chat.

"Well," I say, "after knocking out my column each day, I enjoy a few sets of tennis or maybe I relax at home with a good book and . . ."

Then Mike Wallace interrupts me and says, "That's enough beating around the bush, Mr. Grizzard. Why don't you come clean?"

Startled, I begin to stutter. "Wwwwwwhat on earth are you talking about, Mmmmmmike?"

"This," says Wallace, holding a copy of an essay I did in high school on the Clayton-Bulwer Treaty, an essay which won first place in the county literary meet. "Did you actually write this essay without notes, as the rules of the literary meet specified, or did you, in fact, smuggle in your history book and write your essay by copying word for word from the book?"

I'm squirming from side to side in my chair.

"Look at this, Martha," says the guy in Des Moines.

I did, in fact, smuggle in my history book. How else could anybody write five pages on the Clayton-Bulwer Treaty? But how did Mike Wallace? . . .

"You're probably wondering how we found out about this fraud," says Wallace. "We were first contacted by Arthur Norbest, who finished second in that contest and who just happens to be Harry Reasoner's nephew."

I usually awaken before breaking down in front of the cameras, disgracing not only myself but all my family. Not to mention everybody who signed the Clayton-Bulwer Treaty.

Wouldn't it be ironic, I often catch myself thinking, if one day somebody got something on Mike Wallace, like maybe he wet his bed at camp, and then made him squirm before the entire country? That's a better dream than the one I've been having.

***

I have spent more than half my life working for newspapers. Like many other things in this world, our relationship has been one of love and hate. I love newspapers, but I hate it when they misplay their hands.

I have my own ideas about what should and shouldn't be in a newspaper and about how a newspaper should look. I've never found anyone who was particularly interested in my ideas, but I have them nonetheless. You never know when some wealthy eccentric might leave me a major metropolitan daily.

First of all, if I owned a newspaper, I wouldn't run any color. There is something to be said for good ol' black and white. "It's right here in black and white, Gladys," a man says to his wife when he wants to assure her that something is true beyond a doubt. He would never say, "It's right here in orange and green, Gladys."

I would never run stories in my newspaper about how many fatalities the highway patrol is predicting during the holiday weekend. Too gruesome. If you're going to run that kind of story, why not run one where local cardiologists predict how many people are going to croak from heart attack over the same period?

I wouldn't run scoring summaries from hockey games in my newspaper. They don't make any sense.

I wouldn't allow lengthy interviews with twenty-year-old defensive linemen who, given the choice, probably would rather eat a newspaper than attempt to read one.

I would run follow-ups to society marriage announcements in my newspaper: "Mr. and Mrs. Arnold Crampton announce the divorce of their daughter, Heide Mildred Crampton Millingham III, son of Dr. and Mrs. William Harvey Millingham, Jr. Grounds for the divorce were that Mr. Millingham III whomped his former wife on the head with his polo mallet whenever she complained about his riding his pony in the house."

I would tell my movie critics to cool it on all that imagery and symbolism be-bop and just tell the readers whether or not the movie is worth seeing and how the popcorn is where it's playing and what time the darn things starts.

I would allow precious few interviews with artists. They're more boring than twenty-year-old defensive linemen.

I wouldn't give Ted Kennedy any more publicity. Let him take out an ad.

I'd run fewer stories about abortion, dieting, sex after seventy and before seventeen, how to dress if you're a career woman and have decided being married and having kids is not for you, sperm banks and what to do about liver spots. We have Phil Donahue to cover those things.

I would run more stories about little boys who lost their dogs and then found them, and I'd run eighty percent of all political stories next to the comics page.

Finally, I would watch my columnists very closely. They can be real troublemakers.

— 15 —

Are We Missing A Few Cards?

I HAVE ALWAYS SUSPECTED that some of my friends are not sane. Of course, I would never come right out and say that to them, but in the polite South we have several euphemisms for getting the point across. For instance, we might say of such a person that he's not playing with a full deck. Or, she doesn't have both oars in the water. Or, his lights are on, but there's nobody home. Or, his elevator doesn't stop at all floors. Such phrases seem to be more civil than saying, "He's crazier than a billy goat at mating time."

Although I seldom invite such people to my house for fear they might not leave, I keep them on my Christmas card list to demonstrate to the world how open-minded I am. Besides, in the eternal quest for the origins of true grit and two socks that match, you never know when there might be a gem hiding inside a rock. So, with hammer in hand, allow me to present a few of my rock-headed friends.

***

Not long ago, I decided it was time to invest some of my very small fortune in the stock market (it's the only form of legalized gambling in Georgia). I called my broker friend, Willard "The Bull" Saperstein of Saperstein, Silverman and Simpson, Inc., the brokerage house with the famous slogan, "Yes, yes, yes, buy from SSS."

"Cat food," Willard said the minute he answered the phone.

"Cat food?" I asked.

"Cat food is hot," he said. "More and more people are owning cats these days, and a cat has got to eat."

So I invested heavily in companies that manufacture cat food. A week later, a rumor circulated that Morris the cat had a severe case of indigestion. Nine Lives cat food plummeted two and a half down to just six and a half lives, and the bottom fell out of Puss 'n' Boots as well.

"Just an unlucky break," said Willard, who then suggested that he buy IBM stock for me. IBM has always been a sound company, so I gave him the go-ahead. Sure enough, a week later IBM announced a major breakthrough that sent the stock soaring.

I called Willard and told him to sell, expecting to make a handsome profit on my investment.

"You don't have that IBM," said Willard.

"What other IBM is there?" I asked.

"I bought you International Banjo Makers. It's down eight points and falling fast."

I should have learned my lesson but didn't. Willard soon called with another hot tip.

"American Chinchilla," he said.

"Chinchillas?"

"You should buy every share of American Chinchilla you can get your hands on," said Willard. "It's going to be a cold winter, and there's going to be a heavy demand for chinchilla coats."

It wasn't long before that investment went sour, too, when American Chinchilla discovered that seventy-five percent of the male chinchillas it had bought for its large breeding farm in Oklahoma were gay.

"Don't buy me any more risky stocks," I told Willard.

"Well, why didn't you say so?" He immediately placed an order in my name for one hundred shares of Asbestos Toys. I lost another bundle.

"Get away from me," I said to Willard the next time he called.

"You've just had a few bad breaks," he said. "Give me one more chance and I'll make it all up to you."

Fool that I am, I trusted him once more. Willard came back to me with a new portfolio of can't-miss stocks. He had International Cranberry; a blight killed most of the crop.

He had a new company that had perfected a way to breed worms for fish bait in half the time and at half the cost; one night the worms all crawled out of their boxes and disappeared into the ground.

He had stock in a company that manufactures salt. Salt took a bad health rap. When it rains, it pours.

He had me invest in a company that had developed a chemical that would cure runny nose, itchy throat, stuffy head and that ache-all-over feeling. Unfortunately, it also would inflame your hemorrhoids.

He had Royal Lippizan Stallions, Inc. Several mares came down with herpes and the stallions all had nervous breakdowns.

He had Chrysler. I panicked after all my other stocks fell through the floor and sold two days before it started to soar.

Willard, meanwhile, got out of the stockbroker business.

He's now my bookie.

***

Contrary to what some people have said about me, I don't hate all liberals. I have a very good friend named Blanton who is one of the country's leading liberals.

Blanton is, of course, anti-nuke, except for the one bomb he would like to drop on Ronald Reagan's Civil Rights Commission. He supported George McGovern in '72 but has dropped George like a bad habit in '85. The ticket he would like to see the Democrats offer would feature Jesse Jackson and Jane Fonda. Blanton is against prayer in school, tax write-offs for the rich, capital punishment, boxing, designer clothes and Senator Jesse Helms. He is for passage of the Equal Rights Amendment, the legalization of marijuana, the impeachment of Nancy Reagan, a national holiday honoring John Lennon and giving the Russians the benefit of the doubt.

"You don't agree with President Reagan that Russia is the 'Evil Empire'?" I asked him.

"Conservative claptrap," he answered.

"But what about the Russian invasion and occupation of Afghanistan?"

"Nothing worse than what we did to the American Indians," he said.

I had forgotten about Blanton's interest in the plight of the American Indians. For starters, he wants to give back the land we got in the Gadsden Purchase and make Marlon Brando the new Secretary of the Interior.

What stirs Blanton's liberal blood more than anything, however, is environmental issues. He fought tirelessly to save the snail darter. He has protested vigorously against the slaughter of baby seals. He tried to get chicken put on the endangered species list when a Mrs. Winner's went up next door to a Popeye's in his neighborhood.

Last time I saw Blanton, he was loudly spewing forth his usual tirade against The Right when I asked him what was new.

"Pelicans," he answered.

"Pelicans?"

"Somebody has got to do something for the pelicans in this country."

I had no idea pelicans were in any sort of trouble, but Blanton set me straight.

"Do you know what causes pelicans to die?"

"I don't even know what causes them to get sick," I said. Blanton did not laugh.

"It's the most horrible thing I've ever heard," he explained. What happens is that pelicans have to keep their eyes open when they're diving for fish, and after diving into salt water day after day with their eyes open, they become blind and can't see the fish. Consequently, they eventually die of starvation.

I asked him what we were supposed to do.

"I'm going to Washington to demand that the government provide a pair of goggles for every pelican in America," he said.

Can Blanton save the pelicans? The hell he can. But at least he has a cause, and I know enough about his kind to know this: A liberal without a cause is like, well, a pelican without goggles. What good is a big mouth if you can't find anything to aim it at?

**

Scientists have been trying for years to talk to porpoises, supposedly the most intelligent members of the underwater crowd. Me, I've never understood why there's so much interest. If you could talk to a porpoise, what would you ask him? How's the water?

I once tried to talk to a girl in a singles bar who bore an amazing resemblance to a porpoise. She had a large nose and wore lots of blue eyeshadow.

"What's your sign, sweetheart?" I asked. That one was hot for awhile.

"Pisces," she said.

"I thought so."

"Why is that?"

"Easy," I said. "You look a lot like something that lives underwater." When the swelling went down in about a week, I could see as well as ever.

I really don't find it so incredible that animals might be able to communicate with people. That's because I grew up with the legendary Claude "Goat" Rainwater, who not only smelled like an animal but could also talk to them. Dogs were his specialty. He would talk to any dog in town, except poodles.

"Don't talk to no poodles," said Claude.

"Why not?" I asked.

"Had one once," he explained. "Dog wouldn't talk but one time a year. First year, he said the food I was giving him was bad. After another year, he said he didn't like sleeping outside with the beagles. Third year, he said he wanted to leave and find a new place to live."

"What did you tell him?" I inquired.

"I told him, 'Go ahead. All you've done since you've been here is gripe.' "

Goat also once had a bird dog he bought from a fellow in Texas.

"Dog's a big football fan," said Goat. "Every time he sees a game on television, he raises his paw and says, 'Hook 'em, Horns!' "

"Hook 'em, Horns," incidentally, is the battle cry for University of Texas football fans, a rather rowdy bunch.

I tried to get Goat to make his bird dog do that trick for me, but Goat said it wouldn't be right since it wasn't football season. He said I'd have to wait until the fall. When fall came, however, the dog was gone. Word was he'd been dognapped by a bunch of Oklahoma fans.

I probably didn't miss much anyway. If a drunk Texan can fall off a bar stool in Austin and bellow "Hook 'em, Horns!" twice before he hits the floor, I don't know what's so special about a perfectly sober bird dog being able to do the same thing.

Goat also talked to cows, horses, pigs, chickens and mules. And he also smelled like cows, horses, pigs, chickens and mules.

"Hate trying to talk to a mule," he once said.

"Too stubborn?" I asked.

"Like trying to talk a tomcat into staying home on a Saturday night."

I remember asking Goat what was the most unusual animal he had ever talked to.

"Girl skunk," he said.

"What did she say to you?"

"'What's your sign, big boy?' "

***

My friend Fred was complaining about his children.

"All they do is beg for things and then bellyache if they don't get them," he said.

"What are they begging for?" I asked.

"My son wants a sports car and my daughter wants a trip to Europe."

"How old are your children, anyway?"

"The boys is six," he said, "and the girl is nine."

I used to employ the same strategy with my parents. I'd ask for things like an air rifle, or a Flexy racer or a motor scooter — things I knew they'd never give me. But the idea was to inflate the request so that what I ended up getting was still pretty good.

Actually, I didn't figure out that strategy alone. An older playmate explained it to me one day. I was six at the time and wanted a dog, but my parents weren't ready to take care of one, so they refused. I ran off crying and bumped into the older kid.

"What's wrong?" he asked.

"My parents won't let me have a dog," I sobbed.

"Did you ask them for a dog?" he asked.

"Of course I asked them for a dog."

"Dummy," said my wiley playmate. "That was your mistake. You should have asked them for a little brother. Then they would have given you a dog."

I tried to explain the old ruse to Fred, but he wasn't listening. He seemed preoccupied and generally irritated.

"Come on," I said, "what's really bothering you?"

"Well, it's my fortieth birthday today," he confessed.

"Hey, congratulations! Are you going out tonight to celebrate?" I asked.

"Why should I celebrate?"

"Because it's a milestone in your life, that's why."

"Not to me," said my friend. "It's just another year I didn't get a pony."

***

Rigsby is one of those people who will try anything once. And if he likes it, he'll try it several more times.

He was having dinner at a Mexican restaurant recently when someone suggested a round of straight tequila shooters.

"I'll try anything once," said Rigsby.

He tried one straight tequila shooter, liked it, and proceeded to drink a dozen more. Before finally passing out in his cheese enchilada, he did a Mexican hat dance on the table, sang three verses of "La Cucaracha" and tried to ride a fat lady with shaggy hair because he was convinced she was a burro.

Rigsby has tried sky diving, mountain climbing, square dancing, snake charming, body painting, goat roping and escargot, so I shouldn't have been surprised when he told me he also had tried cocaine. "You know me," he said. "I'll try anything once."

I've never tried cocaine myself, but I'm fascinated by the number of people who apparently think it's worth going to jail for. I asked Rigsby how he came to try it.

"I was at a party," he said, "and somebody introduced me to this fellow from Southern California. He had buttoned up just enough of his shirt so you couldn't see his navel, and he had enough chains around his neck to open a hardware store. We started talking and all of a sudden he looked around the room to see if anybody was watching us. Then he leaned over and asked me if I wanted some coke.

"I told him I'd just stick to the beer, but that there was plenty of Coke and Tab and even some 7-Up in the refrigerator. He thought I was pulling his leg, so he insisted that I come out to his car for a toot. I wasn't sure what a 'toot' was, but you know me — I'll try anything once," continued Rigsby.

"We got to his car and he pulled out one of those bags you wrap sandwiches in. I asked, 'What's in your bag?' He said, 'It's cocaine, man. You want some?' And I said, 'Sure, I'll try anything once.'

"He poured some of it out on this little piece of glass and

then handed me a straw and told me to sniff it up my nose. About two sniffs and I had this powerful urge to sneeze. My sinuses are always giving me trouble, you know. I let out this big one and that cocaine went all over this fellow's car and in his hair. He started cussing me hard and told me I had just blown away $300 worth of cocaine. I said, 'Well, that's show business, Hoss,' and went on back to the party for another beer."

I asked Rigsby if he thought he would ever try cocaine again.

"Once was enough," he said. "But if that fellow paid $300 a sniff for that stuff, I sure would like to meet the man who sold it to him, because, brother, there goes a salesman."

***

My friend Worthington was scared to death when he got the call last week that the boss wanted to see him immediately. He was still shaking when he told me about it.

"Worthington," the boss said, "how are things out in Shipping and Receiving?"

"Fine sir," he said. "We could use an extra forklift, but . . ."

"I'll check into it next week, Worthington. Frankly, I didn't call you in to discuss forklifts. I understand you are the chairman for this year's company Christmas party."

"I am, sir. I'm replacing Van der Meer from Personnel."

"What happened to Van der Meer?"

"He got run over by a forklift."

"What's the damage?"

"Darn thing will probably be out of service for another month, sir. That's why I was saying that we need another forklift."

"I'm not talking about the forklift, Worthington. I'm talking about Van der Meer."

"Oh. He'll be back in a couple of weeks but not in time to

coordinate the Christmas party."

"Well, I know this thing has been practically dumped in your lap, Worthington, but what are your plans?"

"Well, sir, I thought we'd get drunk and chase the secretaries around."

"I'd expect that from somebody in Personnel, Worthington, but you're from Shipping and Receiving. Can't we do something a little more original?"

"Like what, sir?"

"Like drawing names and exchanging gifts."

"Don't you remember, sir? We tried that three years ago, but Whipple from Accounting drew Beulah Riddick from Quality Control and gave her a pair of underpants from Frederick's of Hollywood."

"So?"

"So, Beulah Riddick's husband who worked in Building Maintenance was at the party, and when he saw what Whipple had given his wife, he tried to pull off one of Whipple's ears with a pair of pliers."

"Whatever came of all that?"

"Nothing, really. Beulah and her husband got back together, and if you speak up, Whipple can hear you just fine."

"OK, so forget the gifts. What about we have some coffee and cake and sing Christmas carols?"

"We tried that two years ago, sir, but a couple of the stock boys slipped in some beer and cheap wine, and everybody started throwing cake and a fight broke out and the cops came and the whole thing made the newspapers the next day."

"I seem to remember the headline, now that you mention it, Worthington: 'Workers Deck Each Other in Halls of Local Factory.'"

"You fired Himmerman in Public Relations over that one, sir."

"Himmerman schimmerman. There must be something decent we can do for the annual company Christmas party. What about a dance? We can rent a hall and get a band and have a Christmas dance."

"Tried that last year, sir."

"And?"

"I'm surprised you don't remember, sir. Beulah Riddick got stewed and did a strip number, and when she got down to her unmentionables, her husband started looking for the creep who had given them to her."

"And who was the guilty party? My memory is so bad these days, Worthington. I'm getting on up there, you know."

"Well, sir, Beulah spilled the whole story. You gave them to her."

"Did her husband come at me with those pliers?"

"No, sir. You promoted him to manager of the Houston plant before he had a chance to go out to his truck for his toolbox."

"Worthington?"

"Sir?"

"Let's go with the getting drunk and chasing secretaries. And if I happen to catch one, please remind me what I'm supposed to do next."

***

The majority of my life has been spent either learning to be or being a newspaperman. In the course of that pursuit, I have encountered a plethora of unbelievable and unbelievably talented people.

One such person was John E. Drewry, dean of the Henry Grady School of Journalism at the University of Georgia when I arrived there in the mid-1960's. Founder of broadcasting's revered Peabody Awards, Dean Drewry was a master of the language with a wit that one sees today only in such distinguished gentlemen as Sir John Gielgud and John (Smith-Barney) Houseman.

The Dean wore round glasses that gave him the appearance of an owl, and he wore three-piece suits with a long watch fob hanging from the vest. His accent was aristocratically Southern, making it a joy to hear him pronounce polysyllabic words such as, "im-proh-pri-uh-tee."

As he lectured one day to our class of approximately three hundred students, he walked back and forth across the room that had an exit door to either side of the podium. Each time he reached one of the doors, he would peer out. This routine went on for about forty-five minutes before he offered an explanation.

"Class, I know there are those among you who are wondering why I have made regular visits to each of these doors today, peeking out each time in search of, you are no doubt saying, God knows what. My purpose for this effort is quite simple, my young friends.

"I, as I am sure you have, have become quite interested in our country's missions into outer space. I have said to myself, 'Is it not pompous on the part of all earthlings to consider that we are the only intelligent beings in this universe?' The answer can be only one: of course, it is, and there must be other civilizations out there who, as we are they, are trying to contact us at this very moment.

"Let us consider what might happen if these beings from another planet landed on earth for the first time here on the campus of the University of Georgia. It is certainly not unthinkable that these beings would want first to see the environs of our nation's oldest state chartered institution of higher learning.

"It is further apparent to me," he continued, "that once they removed themselves from whatever contraption it might have been that brought them here, they would first want to visit the School of Journalism where we specialize in the art of communication.

"That being the case, I have been walking to each door today assuming that this might be the day for our first encounter with the extra-terrestrials. Were they to arrive here in our building, I would not want them to have to wander the halls with no one to greet them. As dean, I think that certainly would be my duty."

A couple of years later, when I had taken my college journalism education and put it into practice at the Athens Daily News, I encountered an equally fascinating and talented character in my editor, Glenn Vaughn.

One afternoon when I reported for work, Glenn asked me to step into his office. "What," he asked, "would be the biggest story we could have in this newspaper?"

I thought for a moment before answering. "Coed dorms at the university."

"Bigger than that," said Glenn.

"A four-lane highway to Atlanta."

"Even bigger," he prompted.

"Georgia signs a quarterback who can pass."

"Close," said Glenn, "but that's still not it. The biggest story we could have would be the Second Coming."

I did not argue with him.

"So just in case it breaks while we're here, I've gone ahead and designed page one."

He had the page neatly drawn in green ink on a layout pad. There would be a large file photograph of Jesus on the front, although Glenn was hopeful that the wire services would provide a photo of the actual moment of touchdown. He also had written the headline as well. In bold, 124-point type, it would say, "HE'S BACK!" Underneath that headline would be a smaller one reading, "Details on Page 2."

To this day, I don't know whether Glenn was joking or not.

Billy Bob Robinson was another character spawned by newspapers. He was a member of the Atlanta Journal sports staff when I went to work there in 1968. Robinson's beat was auto racing and outdoors, and he was one of the finest writers in the business...even when he didn't make it to an event. "Never let the facts stand in the way of a good story," was one of Robinson's favorite lines.

Once he wrote a piece about fishing for bass with his good pal, ol' so-and-so down in South Georgia. "Fish are bitin' so good down here," he quoted his friend as saying, "we have to hide the bait to keep 'em from jumpin' in the boat."

Several days after that article appeared, I fielded a phone call in the department.

"Let me speak to that Robinson fella," said the voice on the other end.

"I'm sorry," I said, "but he's out of the office right now."

"Well," said the caller, "just give him a message. Tell 'im that there fella he was supposed to have been fishin' with down here in South Georgia the other day's been dead for six months."

Another Robinson quirk was that he never showed up for work on time. He carried a flat tire around in his trunk to use as an excuse anytime he couldn't think of something more exotic.

Finally the boss told him that if he was late one more time, he would be fired. Sure enough, the next morning Robinson appeared two hours late.

"OK, you know what I told you," said the boss. "You're fired and I don't want to argue about it. But just for the record and for one last time, why were you late?"

"Well," began Billy Bob, "you know that Maria and I have been married for almost nine years and that we have eight children."

The boss nodded in agreement, waiting for the rest of the story.

"Well, this morning was the first time since we've been married that Maria has had a period, and she was too sick to take the kids to school, so I had to do it."

Instead of firing Robinson, the boss took a week off to regain his composure.

***

I had this roommate named Charlie once. We lived in what was basically a dive, but it was our first home away from home, our first taste of independence, so it was special.

We did what all anxious young men do when they first leave the nest — we played our music loud, stayed up late and sought the company of women. I got lucky and met a dazzling young thing. The fact that she had another year of high school left and I was headed off to college seemed to impress her considerably.

I cleaned all the trash out of my car, bought a bottle of English Leather cologne, and even bought a new pair of yellow Gold Cup socks to go with the yellow shirt I planned to wear on our big date. Gold Cup socks were a fashion must in those days. They came in a variety of colors and cost $1.50 a pair, an obscene price even now.

As the time drew near for my date, I showered, shaved

and splashed English Leather all over my body. Then I started putting on the clothes I had meticulously laid out on my bed. But my new yellow Gold Cup socks were missing.

"Have you seen my new yellow Gold Cups?" I yelled to Charlie, who was watching "Bonanza" in the living room.

"Haven't seen 'em," he answered, never taking his eyes off the screen as Hoss Cartwright thrashed a man to within an inch of his life.

I never found those new socks, and my date turned out to be a total bust. I don't know if one was the result of the other, but I spent a good deal of the evening pulling up a stretched-out pair of white socks.

More than twenty years later, I was speaking at a public gathering when a woman came up and asked me if I remembered Charlie, my old roommate.

Of course, I told her.

"Well," she said, "he's a friend of mine, and when I told him I was going to see you here tonight, he asked me to bring you something."

She reached into her pocketbook and pulled out a pair of yellow Gold Cup socks.

"Charlie said he stole a pair of these from you once, and it's been worrying him ever since. He said to give you these and ask you to please forgive him."

I don't wear yellow socks anymore, but there's a pair in my sock drawer anyway.

— 16 —

Grit Is In the Eye
Of the Beholder

A Little Old-Fashioned Justice

IT WAS ALAN'S BIRTHDAY. He met his girlfriend for lunch and they had a few drinks, and then a few more, and then she gave him his presents, one of which was a bouquet of flowers. They had one more for the road before she went back to work and Alan headed home.

On the way, a policeman pulled him over. "Have you been drinking?" he asked.

Alan admitted to having a couple at lunch with his girlfriend. "It's my birthday," he added.

The policeman apologized for ruining Alan's birthday, but he told him he obviously was too drunk to drive, so he loaded Alan into the back of the patrol car.

"I don't know why I did it," Alan explained later, "but I decided to take my flowers with me."

At the police station, they booked Alan for drunken driving and put him in a cell with several others. Again, he took his flowers.

"As they were opening the cell door for me," Alan said, "I realized I shouldn't have brought the flowers with me. One fellow yelled right away, 'Hey, Flower Boy, did you bring those for me?'

"There was a group of black guys sitting in one corner of the cell. When I looked at them and smiled, they smiled back, so I went and sat down with them and tried to make friends," said Alan.

"I told them it was my birthday and that my girlfriend had given me the flowers. They sang, 'Happy birthday, dear Flower boy.' I've never been so embarrassed and so scared in my life. I tried again to make friends.

"I asked one guy what he was in for. He said he was hungry and didn't have any money, so he went into a convenience store and put a can of Spam in his pocket and walked out. He said he didn't even get a chance to eat it before the police stopped him and brought him in with the Spam still in his pocket."

Alan spent the night in jail. At his hearing the next morning — both he and his flowers were somewhat wilted from the experience — the judge was hard on him despite his first-offender status. He received a hefty fine and was placed on probation.

"I learned my lesson," he said. "The quickest way to get people to stop drinking and driving is to make them spend a night in a jail cell holding on to a bouquet of flowers. It's a frightening experience."

Alan was released along with the man who had stolen the can of Spam. "I thought it was a nice gesture," he said. "They gave him the can back."

A citizen learns his lesson about drinking and driving and the Spam bandit, hungry enough to steal for his supper, is allowed to eat the evidence. Just a little old-fashioned justice goin' round.

LOYALTY EVEN UNDER DURESS

Tom first met blue-eyed Mary nearly forty years ago when they both were students at Auburn University. They eventually married and had three daughters and a son.

The family settled in a small Alabama town where Tom began a successful business. Mary took care of the kids and dreamed of finishing her degree, which had been cut short by the kids. Maybe when they were grown . . .

Three of their children ended up with degrees from Auburn, and the family became loyal supporters of the school and especially of the football program. Mary was the biggest War Eagle fan in the entire family. She often clipped headlines about her beloved team and taped them to the refrigerator door.

When the kids had finished their educations, Mary decided it was time to fulfill her dream of returning to school. "School's so hard when you get as old as I am," she told friends, but she wanted that degree. Her grades were high and her family and friends were proud of her.

It all came on suddenly. One day Mary was bounding with energy and enthusiasm; the next day she was in the hospital after suffering a heart attack. A week later, she died at age fifty-seven.

As a friend of the family, I attended the funeral. The preacher talked about how much Mary loved that family but about how she also was her own person: "Completing her education was so important to her," he said. He also talked about her love for Auburn University: "She was fanatical," the preacher said lovingly, and the family even broke into smiles as they remembered the woman's loyalty.

As they rolled Mary's casket from the church, the family followed it down the aisle. Tom held to one of his weeping daughters, trying to comfort her. As he passed, I couldn't help noticing the tie he had chosen to wear to his wife's funeral. On the front, in blue script, were the words, "War Eagle."

"At first," one of the children told me later, "we couldn't believe Daddy was wearing that tie to Mama's funeral. But then, it just sort of made sense somehow."

Yes, it did. It certainly did.

ONE VOTE FOR A POKE

Jason, who is eleven, was walking home from school with a friend. They were doing what all kids that age do — walking through vacant lots, throwing rocks and dirt bombs, "anything to get dirty," his mother said.

Behind a convenience store, Jason accidentally stepped on a board with a rusty nail protruding through it. The nail penetrated his shoe and lodged in his foot. In such excruciating pain, Jason could not get the nail out of his foot, so his friend had to pull it loose.

Bleeding badly and still in pain, Jason limped into the store, showed the clerk his wound and asked for a Band-Aid or some sort of bandage.

"Yeah, I got plenty of Band-Aids," said the clerk. "But have you got a dollar?"

Jason said he didn't have any money, and neither did his friend.

"Sorry," said the clerk. "No money, no Band-Aids."

There was no money for the telephone either, so Jason, still bleeding but aided by his friend, limped the half-mile home.

His mother rushed him to the doctor's office, where he received a tetanus shot. He spent the rest of the weekend hot-soaking his foot. Jason will be fine, but his mother may never be the same again.

"I know now how wars start," she said, "how people get murdered, how hate grows from a tiny little thing into a monster. Ever since this happened, I have wanted to walk into that store and poke that man's eyeballs out. I have wanted to stay home from work and march in front of that store with signs saying, 'Do not buy anything from this store; you might bleed to death.'

"So far I haven't poked anyone's eyeballs out, and to my husband's relief I haven't picketed the store, either. I haven't even called the company to complain; they'd probably just tell me the man was doing his job. I did pray for the man, but I worry about this rage I can't shake.

"You've seen those containers near cash registers that say, 'Take a penny, leave a penny.' Well, I've given enough pennies in this same neighborhood store to buy a large box of Band-Aids. And I would have gladly paid for anything Jason used. I would have appreciated it if the clerk had even allowed him in the bathroom to pack his shoe with toilet paper. And I certainly would have appreciated it if he had called me so I could have picked up my injured child.

"I'm just a mother whose child has been done wrong, and I just don't know about people sometimes. . . . I just don't understand, and I don't know that I ever will."

Me either. And, Lord, forgive me for wishing she had gone for the guy's eyeballs just once.

A DEAL IS A DEAL, SOMETIMES

A man was walking along the river that flows behind a

expensive neighborhood when three guys told him he was trespassing. He argued briefly, but when one of them pulled a gun, he left and went for the police.

He returned later with a police cruiser following him. Behind the police car just happened to be eighteen-year-old Nuno de Almeida, a native of Portugal who had recently come to live with his American-born stepfather.

The man in the lead car stopped when he reached the scene of his trouble and spotted two of the guys who had pulled the gun on him. The police car then stopped, and so did Nuno de Almeida. Suddenly, the police cruiser backed up and crashed into the front of Nuno's car. The cop jumped out of his car, rushed to Nuno's window and accused him of following too closely.

The cop called his sergeant, who arrived on the scene a few minutes later. They conferred and then told Nuno that if he would forget the whole thing, there would be no ticket for following too closely and no chance of losing his license.

Nuno wouldn't make the deal. His car was damaged, and there was still his stepfather to answer to. The two fellows who had pulled the gun had witnessed the whole event. The cop walked over to them, mentioned they could be in big trouble, and asked if they had seen the accident.

"The inference was there," said one of the fellows named Kenny, "that if we backed him, he wouldn't do anything about the gun."

So Kenny and his buddy said they hadn't seen anything. No charges were filed against them for the incident with the gun. The fellow in the lead car also said, truthfully, that he hadn't seen anything.

Nuno de Almeida was given a court date. His stepfather, despite the advice of three lawyers to forget the matter and take the fine, urged his son to fight. "Nuno doesn't lie," he said.

Nuno pleaded not guilty. The policeman gave his side of the story, then Nuno told his version.

"Are you saying the officer is lying?" asked the judge.

"He hit my car when he backed up," said Nuno.

The courtroom laughed. Kenny was then called to the witness stand to testify against Nuno. A deal is a deal. Nuno looked to be in big trouble. It was his word against the cop's and the cop had a witness.

But Kenny and his friend had talked things over. "We just couldn't live with our consciences if we didn't tell the truth," he said. "Why should this kid look like a liar when he wasn't?"

Kenny told the judge the truth about what had happened, that Nuno was not lying. The courtroom broke into applause. The judge dismissed the charges. The officer was left to his superiors.

Only in America.

A LESSON IN SAVING

Brad, age eight, and his sister Linda, age eleven, recently received gifts of fifty dollars each from their grandparents. Brad wanted to spend his money on candy; fifty smackers will buy a lot of Reese's Cups. Linda wanted to spend hers on rock tapes; fifty dollars worth should keep her gyrating till she's sixteen.

Brad and Linda's mother, however, didn't want her children blowing their first serious amounts of money on frivolity. "I wanted them to use their money to learn a lesson," Karen said. "I convinced them that the way to accomplish the American dream was to put their money in a savings account. I explained that the bank would pay them for using their money."

The kids agreed, and so the next morning they all headed down to the bank to open an account. At the bank, however, the kids were told they couldn't have their very own savings accounts because the minimum amount needed was one hundred dollars. Bank policy, it was explained to Karen.

She tried to talk them into pooling their money and opening a single account, but sibling rivalry won out and the kids wouldn't go for that.

A few days later, the grandparents heard of the ordeal, were impressed and decided to give each child another fifty dollars so they could have their own savings accounts. Back to the bank.

This time they were told that Brad and Linda couldn't open their own accounts because they didn't have social security numbers. "The government is afraid somebody will make some interest and they won't get any of it," explained a bank official. Frustrated for a second time, the kids burst into tears.

"I didn't know what to tell them after that," said Karen. I thought teaching the children to save now would make them more likely to do the same when they were older."

To try to make amends to the kids, Karen took them on a shopping spree for candy and rock tapes. It was the only thing left to do. Besides, the children will learn another valuable lesson about money: Easy come, easy go.

17

From Sea To Shining Sea

AS I'VE TRIED TO demonstrate, true grit is not indige-nous to any group or any place. Some of the best examples of the developing and the finished product I've seen, for instance, appeared in Italy.

I was there for three weeks of R&R (Note to IRS agents: That stands for Research and Reflection. I worked night and day, as this chapter proves, and that's why I was forced to list the trip as a deduction). Like most tourists, the first challenge I had to face was the language. To better prepare myself, I bought one of those Berlitz guides of "two thou-sand helpful phrases."

They were right. The guide would have been very help-ful. . . if I had been having a convulsion. The way to say, "I am having a convulsion," in Italian is, roughly, "Io ho le convulsioni." But who's got time to look it up if they're having a convulsion face down in the pasta? If they really wanted to be helpful in those books, they would tell you how to say, "Last night I went out and got drunker than a four-eyed Italian dog, and I desperately need something for this hangover." I couldn't find that phrase anywhere. And I needed it. Bad.

The book did provide me with a useful phrase for the train. The way to say, "I think you are in my seat," is, "Penso che questo sia il mio posto." What it didn't do, however, was tell me what to say when the fellow in my seat was the toughest hombre in Genoa, and he replied with an Italian phrase which I interpreted to mean, "One more word out of you, salami-face, and I'll slice you up like so much prosciutto."

What I finally did was what most Americans do when they can't speak the language. I started using American-Italian, which means putting a vowel on the end of each English word and waving your arms a lot. For instance, if you want to say, "You are standing on my foot," in Italian, you say, "Youo areo standingo ona mya foota." If you look down and point at your foot, it will helpo.

Italians, to their credit, will attempt to speak English with you, thus making it easier for visitors in their country. There is a problem here, too, however: Italians, especially taxi drivers and waiters, know only certain English phrases, and they use them for a multitude of responses.

"If you don't slow down," you might say to the taxi driver, "you are going to kill us all!"

To which he will reply, "Dank you berry much."

Or, to your waiter you say, "This soup is rancid."

"Meddy Chreestmas," he replies.

All the communications problems I had in Italy reminded me of a similar qroblem Bogator Green, the world famous mechanic from my hometown, once had. An Italian couple was driving through in a rental car when it developed engine trouble. A local deputy sheriff came to their rescue and had the car towed to Bogator's "garage," a large shade tree behind his trailer.

The couple spoke no English, and Bogator was only slightly better versed in Italian. After checking their car, Bogator said, "Your manifold's busted."

The man shook his head in bewilderment.

"He's Italian, Bogator," said the deputy sheriff. "He doesn't understand you."

"Oh," said Bogator. He then cupped his hands around his mouth and screamed in the man's ear, "YOUR MAN-IFOLD'S BUSTED!"

***

Once you've mastered the language, another way Americans build character in Italy is by walking the streets.

"You go out for a walk?" asked the bellman at my hotel in Rome.

"Yes," I replied.

"Be careful," he suggested. "The drivers are very aggressive here." And the Pope is Catholic, he might have added.

In a matter of minutes, I had figured it out — it was a game of demolitionio derbyo. The buses try to run over the cars. The cars try to run over what seems to be everybody and his Italian brother on a motor scooter. And all three try to run down the helpless pedestrians, who are nothing more than human bowling pins. The taxi driver who drove me from the train station to my hotel narrowly missed picking up a 7-10 split on the Via Condetti, and he left an easy spare on the Via Veneto when a shopper dived away from his speeding taxi just in time.

"An Italian taxi driver," said another man at the hotel,

"would try to run over his grandmother if she got in his way." I guess that explains the shortage of Italian grandmothers I noted in Rome. I finally figured out that red lights are merely for decoration in Italy, brakes routinely last 100,000 miles since they're seldom used and the quickest way to become rich is to open a body and paint shop.

"Why do people drive this way in Rome?" I asked the bellman.

"Because," he laughed, "ninety-five percent of the Italian people think they are Beppe Gabbiani."

"Beppe Gabbiani?" I asked.

"Richard Petty, to you."

That cleared it up nicely.

***

In Florence, my traditional American values were challenged on every corner. You see, there are a million statues in Florence, and every one of them is naked.

There's "David" by Michelangelo, a masterpiece completed in 1504 when the artist was only twenty-five years old. David makes Bo Derek look overdressed.

There's "The Rape of the Sabine Women" by Giambologna. Children under seventeen must be accompanied by a parent or legal guardian to get a gander at this one.

"Hercules and Diomedes" by Vincenzo de Rossi apparently is a tribute to the sport of wrestling. If you liked watching Argentina Rocca throw Lou Thesz out of the ring, you'll adore "Hercules and Diomedes."

"Perseus" by Cellini is another example of a woman losing her head over a man, and "Bacchus's Fountain" is a sculpture of a fat man riding a turtle. Must be some sort of tribute to Italian turtle racing.

We are not accustomed to such rampant nudity in the United States, and any time it appears, there is always some group stepping forward to protect us. I remember when Marvin Knowles, a fellow from my hometown, made it big in professional wrestling. Using the name "The Masked Pork Chop," Marvin wrestled in National Guard armories and high school gymnasiums as far away as Tupelo, Mississippi.

Because of the acclaim he brought to our town, the local ladies club arranged for "Marvin Knowles Day," which would feature the unveiling of a statue of Marvin in his ring crouch, to be placed on the elementary school ballfield where Marvin got his start wrestling Cordie Mae Poovey, the ugliest and meanest girl in town. The day before the unveiling, however, some of the ladies dropped by to inspect the statue and were shocked to find Marvin wearing nothing but his wrestling tights. They had the sculptor back the next morning before dawn, carving Marvin a pair of loose-fitting underdrawers that reached all the way down to his wrestling boots.

I think maybe they were right. Try as I may, I just can't picture Stonewall Jackson on his horse in the town square wearing nothing but his sword. It ain't fittin'.

***

By the time I reached Venice, I was delighted to hear Americans talking at a table beside me during dinner. It was an elderly couple grappling with noodles and salmon and drinking white wine from a pitcher. I asked where they were from.

"Massachusetts," said the lady, obviously someone's grandmother.

"Originally from Arizona, though," her husband added. He had the look of an ex-soldier.

Apparently they also were glad to hear a voice from home, and we swapped stories over dinner that night. They

223

were both widowed, the lady said, but had been friends back in Arizona before their mates had died. Living alone had not appealed to either of them, so they had married recently. Their eyes met and stayed together as she talked about their marriage.

"So this is a honeymoon?" I asked.

"Just a nice, long trip," the man said. I think I noticed a blush as he spoke. He had started slowly in the conversation, but now the wine was beginning to take effect. They were to be in Europe for three months, he said. First they had visited Germany, then it was on to Austria. The old man told me about the archbishop who once ruled over Salzburg.

"He built a large house," he explained. "And why would an archbishop need such a large house? For the woman he kept there who gave him fifteen illegitimate sons!"

The old man roared with laughter. There's at least a spark left there, I thought.

"Newspaperman," I answered when they asked. The old man brightened again. What a coincidence, he said; his brother-in-law used to be a newspaperman, too.

"He was the music critic for the Washington Post, the one Harry Truman threatened to kick where you don't want to be kicked when he questioned Margaret Truman's musical talents. Years later, my brother-in-law was visiting Independence, Missouri, and was going through the Truman library. Somebody recognized him and asked if he would like to say hello to the former President. Well, of course he would, and do you know what Truman said to him?"

No, I couldn't imagine.

"He said my brother-in-law was right all along. He said his daughter Margaret really didn't have much talent as a musician." The man roared again with laughter.

It was getting late. The man started into the story about the archbishop again.

"You've already told that one, dear," his wife said.

I offered my goodbyes and said maybe we would see each other again sometime. Of course, we wouldn't, but Americans always tell each other that sort of thing. As I left, I heard the man ask his wife, "One more half-liter of wine before bed?"

"OK, let's have one more half-liter," she answered, smiling at him.

Oh, to be young — relatively or otherwise — and in love as night falls on Venice. Or even on Cleveland.

***

I can't think of anything, short of gun-totin' federal marshalls, that would make me move out of the United States. But if for any reason I ever had to pick another country to live in, I think it would be Switzerland.

In the first place, it's a naturally beautiful country with mountain peaks and crystal clear lakes. It's also very clean, the banks are discreet, it's a nice place to shop for cheese and watches and the taxi service is wonderful.

Most of the cabs in Switzerland are late model Mercedeses or BMWs. I've ridden in taxis in the U.S. that were so old the driver had to pull off the road to reshoe his mule. Also, when a taxi picks you up in Switzerland, the driver gets out and opens the door for you. In the U.S., most taxi drivers are surlier than Mr. T with a bad case of hemorrhoids and wouldn't open the door for their grandmother if she were carrying a steamer trunk.

Here are some other nice things about Switzerland:

• When you cross the street, motorists stop and allow you to pass. In most American cities, it's open season on pedestrians.

• When you swim in a Swiss pool, you must wear a bathing cap. I asked the pool attendant why. "You shouldn't have to swim with other people's hair floating in the water," she said. Darn straight.

• There are very few billboards along the Swiss roadways. You can actually see the countryside.

• While I was in Switzerland, I didn't see a single snake or mosquito.

• The air in Switzerland doesn't burn your nose, and when the temperature reaches eighty, they think they're having a heat wave.

• I don't think they have much of a crime problem in Switzerland, either. I base this assumption on an experience I had in Lugano. I noticed a man down on his hands and knees drawing a beautiful picture of the Virgin Mary on the sidewalk with colored chalk. Around the man were several shoe boxes in which those who appreciated his artwork had dropped coins. The following evening I happened to pass by the same spot. The artist was gone, but the shoe boxes were still there along with the day's collection. "You mean to say," I asked a native, "that he can leave his coins out there all night and nobody will steal them?" The man looked shocked. "Steal from a poor artist?" he asked. "Who would steal from the poor?"

That's another thing I like about Switzerland: It still has a ways to go to catch up with the rest of civilization.

***

Of course, if Italy or even Switzerland isn't your cup of wine, there are many other options for interesting vacations closer to home which can also teach you about the world and the wonderful characters who populate it. Here are just a few American vacation packages I could recommend:

• GALA ARKANSAS — Four days and five nights in the

"Land of the Razorback." Learn to stand on a table in a restaurant and scream, "Soooooooooie Piiiig!" like the happy University of Arkansas football fans do when they go out of town. Learn to jump-start a pickup truck like the University of Arkansas football fans do when they try to get back home. Visit the lovely Ozarks and stay in a real mountain shack near Dogpatch, USA. See firsthand what outdoor plumbing is all about! The kids will love it! (Soap, towels, heat, lights, snakebite kits and ammunition NOT included.)

• THE OTHER FLORIDA — Tired of crowded beaches and fancy hotels? Then this might be just right for you. A trip off Florida's beaten paths to lovely, exciting Bugspray Swamp Resort, located in the mysterious Everglades. Explore the hidden world of reptiles and insects with guide, cook and medicine man. Take a hike in Quicksand Alley. (Who got left behind?) See mosquitoes the size of eagles and gnats as big as bats. Four days, five nights and six chances out of ten that at least one member of your family gets eaten by an alligator.

• OLD SOUTH TOUR — Get a real feel for the Old South with a tour of Fort Deposit, Alabama, and meet Fort Deposit's leading citizen, Billy Bob Bailey, and his dog, Rooster. See the local diner where Governor George Wallace once had lunch during a campaign trip. See the local hospital where the governor recuperated. Visitors from New Jersey and other places Up North will want to ask Billy Bob about his special deals on souvenirs, like water actually carried by soldiers during the Civil War, dirt from historic Civil War battlefields and trained boll weevils. And, if you're lucky, Rooster might even do some tricks for his northern friends, like removing their distributor caps. Don't worry. Billy Bob's Service Station, located next to the souvenir shop, is open twenty-four hours a day.

● NUDE BEACH — Just think of it! Nude swimming, nude tennis, nude golf and nude volleyball. And we know just the rock you can hide behind to see it all. Film extra.

● DINOSAUR WORLD — Located off Highway 78 near beautiful downtown Snellville, Georgia. Huge replicas of dinosaurs and other prehistoric animals. Great fun for the kids and educational, too. Would you like to own Dinosaur World yourself? Ask for Harvey and make him an offer. Any offer.

● DUDE RANCH — Here's a dude ranch with a new twist. Instead of riding a bunch of smelly horses, ride dinosaurs and other prehistoric animals. Located off Highway 78 near beautiful downtown Snellville, Georgia. Tell Harvey, the dude who got stuck with this joint, to "saddle 'em up!"

***

If your tastes run more to the great outdoors, I could recommend a rafting trip down the raging Colorado River. But before you sign up for such an arduous undertaking, you may want to ask a few questions — to which I already have the answers.

1. How do I get to the Colorado River? Fly from Las Vegas out into the middle of the Arizona desert in a small airplane (envision a '53 Ford with wings) and land in a wide place between two cacti. Then ride a mule down the treacherous ledges of the canyon to the river and pray the mule doesn't make one false step, because mules, unfortunately, don't have wings.

2. How can the Arizona desert best be described? Ten zillion acres of dust.

3. Is there ever a change of scenery? Occasionally you see a cow pie.

4. Once on the river, are the rapids exciting? Lie down on a water bed and get a small child to jump up and down on it. Same thing, except you don't get as wet.

5. How hot is it on the river? During the day, about 120 degrees, but at night it cools down nicely to maybe 102.

6. Where do you camp? On sandy river banks.

7. What is it like camping when the wind starts blowing at night? Think of a blast furnace.

8. What do you eat on the trip? Mostly sand.

9. How did the brochure describe camping at night along the river? "...Drift slowly off to sleep under the starry western skies as you are caressed by a cool breeze, the restful sound of rushing water and the pleasant blend of guitars and mellow voices."

10. Has the person who wrote the brochure ever actually taken the trip? No.

11. Was there anybody interesting along with you? Yes. A newlywed couple on their honeymoon.

12. What do you call people who take a rafting trip down the raging Colorado for their honeymoon? Weird.

13. Did you encounter any scorpions? Yes, but the red ants were worse. Scorpions sting only in self-defense; red ants bite because they enjoy it.

14. What about rattlesnakes? Don't worry. We never found more than one at a time in a sleeping bag.

15. What are the restroom facilities like in camp? A little green tent.

16. What is the most important thing to know about camping on the Colorado River? Never spread your bedroll near the little green tent.

17. Will you ever take such a trip again? Sure, as soon as mules sprout wings and fly.

***

I used to recommend Hilton Head, South Carolina, as a wonderful getaway spot, but not long ago a friend sent me a clipping from the island's newspaper which warned of trouble. For the sake of an informed public, following is a reprint of that article:

Members of an elite corps of South Carolina state militia stormed the beach here Saturday and reclaimed the plush resort from thousands of Northern vacationers who took over the island several years ago after surrendering Miami Beach.

"Hilton Head is a part of the sovereign state of South Carolina," declared Governor Willis Peabody, "and nobody else has any right to any part of the soil our forefathers grabbed off the Indians. Any attempt to retake the island will result in the gravest of consequences."

The governor would not elaborate on what he meant by "gravest of consequences," but the South Carolina militiamen have put the island under what some of the Northern vacationers are referring to as "the next thing to martial law." One new order disallows the sale of piña colada mix to anyone who cannot prove he or she was born south of Richmond, Virginia.

Hilton Head Island, with miles of beach, numerous golf courses and tennis courts and Ralph Lauren's coastal headquarters, is just off the South Carolina mainland near the Georgia port city of Savannah.

The pre-brunch raid which reclaimed the island was believed to have been launched from Williams' Seafood Restaurant in Savannah in bass boats rented from the Thunderbolt Marina, Bait and Tackle. "We even brought our own beer," said Captain Charlie "Swamp Fox" Ravenel, head of the Carolina militia.

It is believed that the militia also included volunteers from the neighboring state of Georgia, which has had a recent problem with a growing number of Northerners moving into its Golden Isles resorts of Jekyll Island, St. Simons Island and Sea Island. This belief was stimulated by reports that some of the militiamen, upon storming across the beach and reaching the lobby of the Hilton Head Holiday Inn, cried out, "How 'bout them Dawgs!" — a familiar Georgia exclamation for any occasion, including selected funerals.

The Northern-bred occupants of the island, including visitors from the Canadian province of Ontario who were on the island looking for reptile farms and glass-bottom boats, were caught completely off guard by the attack. There apparently was only one casualty, however; a lady from Akron, Ohio, on the beach to catch some early rays, was stepped on by an attacking militiaman and suffered a pair of broken sunglasses.

"You can spot yankee men on the beach from a mile out in the ocean," Captain Ravenel said. "They all wear Bermuda shorts, sandals and black socks pulled up to their armpits. But yankee women, they put on those white bathing suits and they haven't been in the sun in so long, then blend right into the sand. My man said he thought that lady was some kind of jellyfish that had washed up on the beach. If he'd have looked a little closer, he'd have seen her mustache and probably would have missed her."

Reaction came swiftly from the North. One possible retaliatory move, said Governor Fitzhugh Stratsworth III of Ohio, was to move the Ohio National Guard south to Hilton Head to meet the Carolina militia head-on. "If we don't have to stop every time somebody has to go to the bathroom, we could be in the Hilton Head area in three to four days," Governor Stratsworth said.

Meanwhile, Secretary of State George Schultz has already landed in Hilton Head and announced that he is prepared to "stay as long as necessary" to help mediate the dispute. Told at a ninth-hole briefing that rumors were flying that the Carolina militiamen were feeding some of the yankee inhabitants to the many alligators that live on the island, Schultz quipped, "I thought they only ate grits."

*** *

Not long ago I was strolling down New York's Fifth Avenue with a native. He pointed out things I'd never thought to observe before.

"Watch the Japanese tourists," he said. "They'll take pictures of anything, even the sky."

That made sense to me. I explained to the New Yorker that in most other parts of the world the sky is blue, and that the visitors from the East probably were intrigued by the fact that the sky in New York has a brownish or yellowish tint to it.

Then my guide told me how to distinguish a native New Yorker from a tourist. "Watch their eyes," he said. "New Yorkers never look up. They either look down or straight ahead. Only visitors to the city look up."

In addition to being bored with tall buildings, I suspected that most natives had suffered some misfortunes with pigeons and therefore did not look up.

My friend further explained that if I watched closely, I would observe that three out of every five New Yorkers would be wearing headsets. "It's our way of dealing with noise pollution," he said.

But if their ears are plugged with loud music, how are they going to hear the two-second blast of the horn which taxi drivers politely give before driving over pedestrians?

Further down Fifth Avenue, my guide showed me yet another point of interest. Along the sidewalk, a crowd gathered to watch large amounts of money changing hands in a little card game being played on top of cardboard boxes. It was like the old shell game: three cards face down, two black and one red. The dealer switches the cards around; the object is to find the red one. I saw people betting as much as a hundred dollars.

"Don't get involved," said my friend. "The people you see winning are shills for the dealer. The tourists see them win and so they give it a try, but they almost always lose."

"Isn't that illegal?" I asked.

"Of course, it is," said the native, "but they have lookouts for the police. If a cop heads their way, they simply grab their box and go to another street."

"You said tourists almost always lose. Does that mean some occasionally win?"

"Yes and no," he answered. "If they do happen to win, one of the shills follows them down the street, mugs them and gets the money back."

About that time we passed a group of Japanese tourists. I nodded and said hello to them. They all took my picture as if I were unusual.

***

They told me about Old Faithful, the world-famous geyser that's the main attraction at Yellowstone National Park in Wyoming, when I was a kid in school. I wasn't much impressed. So every hour on the hour this hole in the ground spews out a lot of steam and hot water. That's a big deal?

Rock City and Disneyland certainly were on my list of things to see when I could afford it, but Old Faithful wasn't in the running. My traveling companion through the wilds of Wyoming, however, had a different idea.

"People come from all over the world to see it," he explained. "We're crazy to come this far and not get a look at it."

I checked the map. We were 120 miles roundtrip from Yellowstone. "You want to drive that far just to see hot water and steam?" I asked. "Why don't you just turn on the shower and close the bathroom door tonight?"

He responded by questioning my patriotism, so the next thing I knew we were on our way to Yellowstone, where bears eat people, to see Old Faithful. We arrived just after eight o'clock.

My friend explained that since a major earthquake in the area in 1983, Old Faithful — which previously had been spewing forth on the hour for more than a hundred years — was running as much as eighty-two minutes between eruptions.

"You mean we've come this far and the thing might not even go off?" I complained.

"It'll go off," he said. "That's why they call it Old Faithful."

There must have been three thousand people sitting on

benches patiently waiting for the show. Me, I went for an ice cream cone.

"You might miss it," warned my friend.

"So I'll see the highlight film," I quipped.

When I came back with my cone, Old Faithful was smoking a little steam but nothing more. The crowd still waited quietly. Then, at about half past eight, it happened. There was steam, and more steam, and then there was a roar and I think the ground trembled. Old Faithful belched forth with a boiling, steamy column of water that reached over a hundred feet into the sky.

The crowd gasped in awe. The explosion seemed to go higher and higher, and when it ended a few minutes later, the crowd fell silent for a moment before bursting into spontaneous applause.

Later, as we were driving in the darkness of the park, my friend asked me how I felt when I saw Old Faithful come through for her audience.

"Proud to be an American," I answered.

I can't explain why. You just had to be there.

***

From New York to Dallas, from Florence to Yosemite, there are men, women and children walking around with hearts full of true grit. It may be hidden beneath the surface of poverty or tattoos or behind the face of wrinkles, but it's there just the same, pure and clear.

So what if they might be riding Shetland ponies instead of gallant steeds? They all could have ridden alongside Marshall Rooster Cogburn, hallowed be his name and theirs.

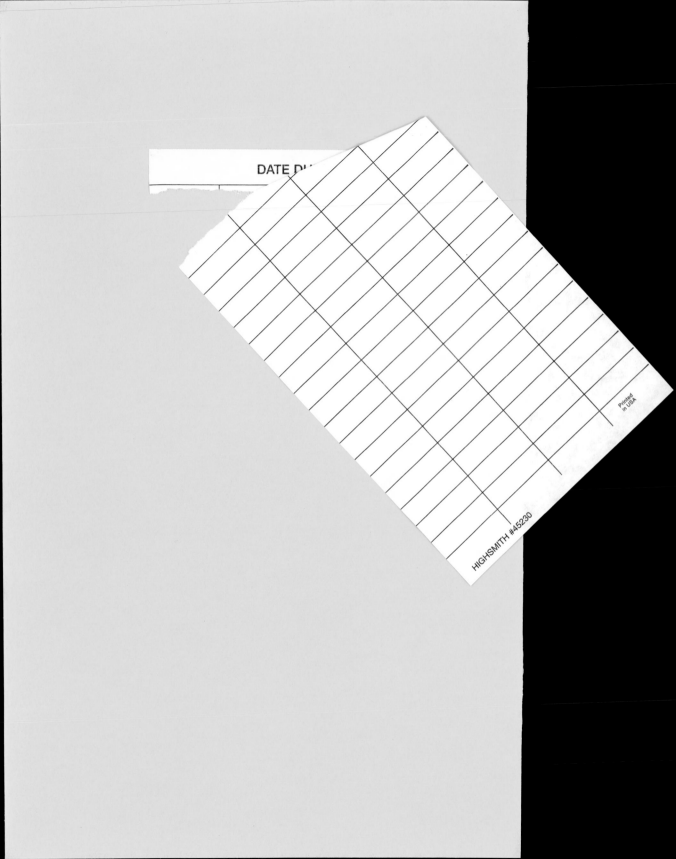

DATE DU

HIGHSMITH #45230

Printed
in USA